The Language of Parenting

The Language of Parenting

BUILDING GREAT FAMILY
RELATIONSHIPS AT ALL AGES

David M. Frees III

Red Wire Press
Ideas and information to improve your life

Malvern, PA

A portion of the profits of this book will be donated to Chester County Community Foundation, a community foundation, to support local philanthropy and good works including support of the Community Coalition. The Community Coalition is an economic association of grass-root, non-profit organizations who collaborate to streamline fundraising so more of every donated dollar goes straight to work creating jobs, homes, day-care, advocacy and a full community life for all of our neighbors. For more information, about this model please call 610-415-1167, or look up their Web site: www.thecommunitycoalition.org.

David Frees would also like to thank the staff at the Jenkins Group, Inc. for their guidance during the book production process.

Published by Red Wire Press
P.O. Box 507
Malvern, PA 19355
www.redwirepress.com

Publisher's Cataloging-in-Publication Data
Frees, David M.

> The language of parenting : building great family relationships at all ages
> / by David M. Frees. –Malvern, PA : Red Wire Press, 2003.
>
> p. ; cm.
>
> ISBN 0-9729647-0-3
>
> 1. Parenting. 2. Parent and child. 3. Child rearing. 4. Communication in the family.
> I. Title.

HQ769.F74 2003   2003091993
649.1—dc21   0306

Project coordination by Jenkins Group, Inc. • www.bookpublishing.com
Cover design by Ann Pellegrino
Author photo credit: David Campli
Interior design by Barbara Hodge

Printed in the United States of America

07 06 05 04 03 * 5 4 3 2 1

Dedication
I dedicate this book to Robin, Josh, Jamie, and Alex. I love you all.

Contents

Disclaimer

This book is designed to help great parents become even better. It is intended to help you take responsibility for changing and improving your life. To that end, it presents an abundance of intellectual nutrition and mental exercises that are, in some cases, scientifically tested. Other material merely represents the opinion of the author or constitutes observations based on the experience of the author and other contributors. However, the interaction of children and their parents is complex, individual, and highly varied. This book does not address physical or mental health problems and is certainly not intended to replace professional, medical, psychological, or psychiatric advice. Every parent/child relationship is different. And every such relationship is in constant change. Parenting is a process. The author encourages you to examine, think about, and utilize the principles and strategies as well as the tactics of communication discussed in this book. However, each person must act responsibly and must, whenever necessary, consult a counselor, psychologist, or psychiatrist. The publisher expressly disclaims any responsibility for any losses or risks incurred as a consequence of the application of the content of this book. In other words, enjoy communicating with your children, use your head, and learn to trust your gut.

A Note About Grammar

This is a book about powerful communication skills disguised as a book about parenting. It is also a book about enhancing verbal communication between the generations, and improving the relationships between parents and children of all ages. Because there are significant differences between optimal verbal communication and writing, especially the more formal kinds of writing, you may find examples of grammatical or "stylistic" errors. You should know that care has been taken in the editing to conform the book to the rules of grammar whenever possible.

However, because there are portions of this book, which are meant to be read aloud or read to oneself, and because the book attempts to model examples of effective verbal communication, it contains several intentional errors. In fact, it is the very violation of the rules of formal style and grammar, which, in some cases, contributes to the high level of effectiveness of communication. Enjoyable and effective communication is often, but not always, pleasing to the ear. Sometimes it is meant to shock, or make one question and consider a statement more thoroughly. I wanted to alert the "editor types" among you to this so that you can enjoy the book and use the techniques without nitpicking about style.

"The greatest discovery of any generation is that a human being can alter his life by altering his attitude."

—William James

Acknowledgments

I would like to say thank you and acknowledge my many teachers who made this book possible. Some were adults and many were children. They include my parents, my schoolteachers who cared enough to instill in me a love of learning, and a number of college and law school professors including Professor Bruce Andrews, Professor Mark Ruhl, and Professor Jan Krasnewicki. I would also like to thank Grand Master Chae T. Goh and Judge Kevin Hess.

There are also many people who contributed ideas, expertise, quotations, and stories. They include: Dottie Walters, Fredrick Wirth, M.D., Peter Goldenthal, Ph.D., Saul Schwarz, M.D. and my wife, Robin B. Frees, IBCLC.

Next I would like to acknowledge and thank my family members—who are patient, supportive, and understanding: My wife, Robin, my kids, Josh, Jamie, and Alex, my parents, Dave and Mary Jane Frees, and my extended family of siblings both natural and by marriage, who tolerate my idiosyncrasies.

Finally, I would like to thank everyone who read and commented upon the book, including Mark Rupp, Eleanor Grant, Frank Mendicino, and Carol Cartaino. Thanks also to my partners, Ross Unruh, Donald Turner, William J. Burke, III, John Fiorillo, John Hall, and Kevin McLaughlin and my staff, Tara Kraft, Nancy Breuer and Douglas Kaune, whose patience and assistance have been invaluable. A special thanks to Tara Kraft for all of her assistance in typing and revising the book. Without her help this book would exist only in my mind or on a pile of tattered legal pads.

Introduction

"The happiest people seem to be those who have no particular cause for being happy except that they are so."

—William Ralph Inge

"Practice being happy for no reason at all."

—Author David Frees

As a parent, have you ever had the experience of real rapport with a child? Can you remember a specific time when you were speaking to that child and the communication was so easy and so clear? Do you remember a time when your child or children understood what you meant, when they were happy, when they answered and acted in a way that made you feel that they unquestionably understood? Do you remember a time when a child spoke to you and his meaning was clear, and even if you disagreed, he seemed respectful? Did it make you feel good as a parent? Do you remember a time like that with your spouse or partner?

These things appear to happen naturally. They don't seem to be planned. These beautiful moments seem to come and go as they please. But I am here to tell you that you help to create them. With a little thought and some practice they can be yours more often. Are you tired of arguing about homework, childrearing, or clothing? With the right attitude, strategies, and the tactics of great communicators, arguing may become almost obsolete. You can still argue with your kids for fun if you want to, but you will not have to.

What is my message to you? It is within your power to transform your life and maybe the world. How? There is a method to great family communication. There are proven principles and strategies, ways to teach, learn, and interact within a family that work more consistently than others.

The more of these principles and methods you know and understand, the more often you apply them, the more willing you are to enjoy teaching and communicating with children, the more you are going to be surprised by how effective your communication can be. You can become addicted to the process of great communication. The more you practice, the more flexible you are, the more you enjoy communication, the better your life begins to feel. Interested?

The principles, strategies, and tactics of great communication discussed in this book are drawn from the experiences of great communicators, and research in the fields of linguistics, general semantics, neurobiology, neurolinguistic programming, psychology, family therapy, anthropology, and other fields. Even as you read these words, neuroscientists, psychologists, and others are working and researching the methods of achieving a happier life through better communication with yourself and others. However, there is nothing new here. You already know how to do all of these things.

For that reason, this book is designed to remind you to work with your conscious and unconscious mind in order to help you to discover, and more frequently reproduce, the ways in which **you are already successful**. As a result, you may do those things more often, achieve more of what you desire, and build your family and parental communication skills. It may seem hard at first or it may even seem effortless. In any case, commit now to doing a better job and to feeling better. The book is a tool. Working with the tool can be really fun. It all depends on how you look at it. Is great communication a job or an adventure? The results of your efforts and of better communication can be priceless. How would it feel to confidently help your children to learn, love school, and to happily join in family activities? Instead of hearing angry or terse communication how would they feel if your communication, by its very nature confirmed that you loved them? Use this book to discover and enhance those feelings.

What are my credentials for teaching you these things? I am not a psychologist or psychiatrist. I am a parent, a teacher, a practicing lawyer, a speaker, a communications consultant, and a perpetual student. I also spend my professional life listening, teaching, and using the skills of master communicators and persuaders. Some people call me a "master communicator." I find that title amusing and I love it that businesses, individuals, and organizations ask me to teach these skills. It also motivates me to keep trying. I mean if somebody calls you a master of anything you better try not to make the really obvious errors too often. I still make mistakes but since I have become more aware and have learned to focus my attention, I make mistakes less often. The things I love the most I then begin to teach.

I teach in seminars and workshops around the world. And wherever I go—down the street or across the world— I invariably find something that fascinates me. I study it, watch it, ask questions about it, listen to what others have to say about it, and pretty soon, if I am lucky, I begin to go beyond confusion and curiosity to learning. I begin to "get it." Once I get it I'm immediately curious about how I can use the new information. I ask myself "How can I use this?"

That is a good question. But "How can this information improve my life?" is better still. "How can that knowledge help me, my family, and others to have a superior life?" is better still. "How can I use this knowledge to easily radically improve my life, my relationships, and my financial wealth?" is better yet. It's nice to ask questions that get your unconscious mind's attention. They're more exciting and therefore more motivating. When you make it a habit to ask yourself better questions, you get better answers and better results. This book is designed to inspire you to ask better and better questions.

For me, that makes things much clearer. I have to organize, reflect, synthesize, and then begin to apply my knowledge. I meet, speak to, and learn from thousands to tens of thousands of people each year. Everyone I meet teaches me something and I am always on the lookout for that "nugget" of information. It is always there. You just have to look for it and ask the right questions.

This book is a **highly condensed** version of some of the lessons I have learned as a student, a lawyer, a teacher, and a parent. Try to keep track of the most valuable "discoveries" you make. Most will not be real discoveries. You may just realize that when you are getting the results you want, you are already using these "discoveries." If you make a discovery, write it down. When that little voice inside says "I do that! Is that what makes it work?" then start using that knowledge more often and watch yourself, listen to yourself, and feel yourself becoming more successful.

As you can already tell, this is not an academic book. It is not based on my own scientific studies. That's okay. I want you to use your own critical faculties. Try the techniques out. Judge each of them for yourself. In fact, much of what you and I will explore is supported by other people's scientific work in the areas of psychology, linguistics, general semantics, neurolinguistic programming, and neurobiology. Occasionally, I will cite the underlying research. If that helps you to feel more confident and to **use this book** then I am delighted. That is my real goal. I hope that some of the things I have been taught, or which I discovered the hard way, through trial and error will be available to you more easily. This book is all about *implementation*. I imagine that results are what you want, too. You want more than a quick read. You bought this book to make your life and the lives of your children better.

My fondest hope is that as a result of your reading, you will begin to enjoy the process of parenting even more. That can happen at any point in life—before your child is born or when your child joins AARP. It is never too late to begin to improve in anything we do. For example, when you smile a little more often you may find that your children, parents, spouse, partner, or others in your life do, too. When communication leads to connection and enjoyment we are doing our job as human beings and as parents.

Finally, the book is organized to be useful. While you are reading or after you have read the whole thing, it is designed to help you implement and act on the strategies that work for you and for your children. Each chapter concludes with a review of the concepts and action items and suggestions.

Some chapters contain exercises. Some exercises are simply thought experiments. They are designed simply to be read and enjoyed; others require more effort on your part. Scientific data does support the idea that these exercises work to create better long- and short-term memory and better, more effective use of the strategies and tactics of communication. So please enjoy reading and doing the exercises.[1] You will become better faster, you will become convinced of the value of this knowledge, and you will be a better model for your own children and other family members. These are worthwhile goals. Read, become aware, practice, and then just forget about it and have fun becoming a better communicator and parent.

> *"Success is shy—it won't come out while you're watching."*
>
> —Author Tennessee Williams

Part One

Building a Foundation

"As to methods there may be a million, but the principles are few. The man who grasps principles can successfully select his own methods. The man who tries methods, ignoring principles, is sure to have trouble."

—Author Ralph Waldo Emerson

Introduction to
Part One

All great achievements require a strong and effective foundation. Part One, which includes chapters on learning, utilizing beliefs, developing the strategies of successful planning, listening, and rapport is the foundation from which your great adventure as a parent and extraordinary communicator will begin. If you have selected this book you probably don't want to be a merely adequate communicator or a somewhat better communicator. I suspect you have more dramatic goals in mind. Begin to move toward those goals by realizing that this book is an undertaking in learning and discovery and that you already have, right inside you, an outstanding method or process for learning and utilizing information. You can begin to improve the process by becoming aware of how you learn now and how you **implement new ideas**. By practicing it, that process will become more effective. You will become more confident and will use the process more often.

This section will also help you to realize that beliefs are the lenses through which we examine and understand the world around us. By becoming aware that we have a choice about our beliefs and that the beliefs we accept and act upon help us to create our experience, we can become radically more effective communicators, parents and teachers. For that reason, we must become more aware of our own beliefs—both the empowering and disempowering ones. Then we can find out where our own beliefs overlap with those of well-known and recognized communication experts. We can examine our own experiences to determine which beliefs have served us well and which beliefs no longer serve us and should be discarded.

Finally, any great undertaking begins with a plan. Planning gives us the courage and ability to move forward and implement our knowledge rather than just understand it. Planning helps eliminate fear and inaction. For that reason, we will examine the formula for success used not only by great communicators, but by successful people in all walks of life from the spiritual to the secular to the financial.

1

Quantum Learning

"Imagination is more important than knowledge"

—Scientist, sailor, author, and philosopher Albert Einstein

W hy begin a book about communication with a chapter on learning? Well, reading this book is a learning exercise. Being a great communicator is a process of ongoing and constant learning. Great communicators are always seeking to discover what interests, motivates, entertains, and persuades the listener. So if you want to get better at communicating with your children and family then taking a few minutes to explore and enhance your own learning model is worth the effort. It will make the experience more effective and enjoyable, won't it? I mean, if you can enhance the usefulness of this book through a few preliminary exercises and by reading a few extra pages before getting to the heart of the matter then that should be a great investment. If not, then skip to Chapter 3—but you'll only be cheating yourself. The rest of us are going to **have a good time here**.

Everyone has a customized learning model that works best for him or her. However every one of us can make our model better and more versatile. In fact, some people have practiced and improved various customized models for the different areas of their lives. We call them "well rounded." They seem pretty happy. Usually they are happy because they have chosen to enjoy being well rounded. Other people have just one well-developed strategy. They seem to do very well in certain contexts but not others. We call them "focused" or we say that they "have a one-track mind."

For example, some people do well in public school because such schools tend to emphasize memorization and reading comprehension. Others do well in sports because they learn game strategies and develop fine and gross motor skills quickly. Some excel at mathematics and engineering. Some of us prefer to read while others prefer to listen. The ways in which we learn are varied. However, there are certain fundamentals of learning that seem to enhance our abilities, our skills, and our acquisition of knowledge no matter how we learn.

Before we begin the process of learning how to communicate with children, spouses, and other family members it is worth a few moments of our time to realize that there are ways to learn and to communicate with yourself that will make this whole game much easier and more enjoyable. Even if you already have a great learning model you can always make it better. And as I always remind my students, once you have developed a better model your stronger, more agile, and newly improved mind is capable of making an even better model and so on.

Furthermore, being able to recognize that someone else's learning style and strategies may be different (even radically different) from your own may be a powerful realization for you. When you realize that your children and the adults around you each have different ways of learning, processing information, and communicating you will become more flexible, patient, and understanding—and therefore more effective. When you realize that others learn in ways that are radically different from your own, you can begin to build a new rapport with them and tailor your communications more specifically to their style and their needs at that moment in time. There is no right or wrong way. Try to enjoy your own way of learning. Try to encourage your children to enjoy their most natural way of learning. Try to encourage curiosity and flexibility in yourself and your children. It is almost always better to employ more than one method of teaching and learning.[2]

Later we will examine the different learning styles and what you should know about them. But for now, let's focus on *your own* way of learning. This is an interactive book. From time to time I'll ask you do an exercise. Studies show that when we are in a relaxed state and learn using more than one of our senses, our long-term retention soars.[3] When you make physical movements (such as writing) during learning as well as when you hear and see the information these multiple activities help you to retrieve (and use) the information more easily. The exercises are also designed to let you experiment with the knowledge. You don't have to believe me. I'll give you an opportunity to try out the information to experience how well it works. You can judge it for yourself.

Awareness Learning Exercise

As you learn, you will usually do something to tag the memories to make them more accessible. Remembering this can be very useful. Can you remember a time when **you learned** something **quickly** and **easily**? When it seemed easy to remember and use the information? Try to remember a specific time. Notice how you were sitting or standing, how you were breathing, what sounds you heard, and whether or not you were making pictures in your mind. These are clues as to how you learn. Remember, as you read, to use those clues. Notice what you were doing when you learned. How did you feel? What did you see? Were you learning to do something physical? Notice the setting. Were you learning something in school? Were you learning something from a parent? Were you learning something from a story?

There are many things to be aware of as you examine these memories of times when you learned quickly and easily. They are sensory clues to the process you use. Begin to notice whether you said anything to yourself or whether others said anything to you. Notice the tone of voice you used and whether or not any external sounds were present. Notice your physiology and posture. Were you sitting, standing, tense, or relaxed when you learned in a way that made you feel good and sure that you would be able to remember? Also, notice if you had any physical or emotional feelings, any particular lightness or heaviness in your body and notice where they were located. All of these "sub-modalities" are clues. Sub-modalities are the various qualities of the visual, auditory, and kinesthetic senses we use to perceive the world and to learn. They are clues to how you learn quickly and easily. By duplicating your state of mind and the feelings in your body (your physiology) you can more accurately re-create this optimal state of learning for yourself. In fact, the very act of remembering peak learning experiences helps to recreate them.

The use of your imagination or your memory can create many of the same electro-chemical reactions in your body, which existed when you actually experienced the peak learning state. Have you ever been to a movie that made you "feel" happy or sad? You were not really experiencing what you saw on the screen. It was not a real experience. Yet watching the movie affected your body. Your mind altered your body's biochemistry. Now that you realize that you can *choose* what feelings to create and intensify, you can begin to choose more often what experiences to focus upon.

If you are aware of how you learn, how you remember, and how you use information, you have become consciously aware of your learning "strategies." When you examine optimal experiences you become aware of optimal strategies. When you utilize these strategies in the course of reading this book and doing the exercises in it you are more likely to find that you will be able to understand the information, remember it, and use it effortlessly and successfully. Also begin to notice how your spouse or partner and children learn. Where is their focus? Can you help them to be in the best frame of mind more often? What kind of a role model are you? Can you do better?

For those of you who are wondering what is going on, I will be a little more explicit. There is a body of knowledge known as neurolinguistic programming or NLP. The founders of NLP, Dr. Richard Bandler and John Grinder, collected and synthesized information from work in cognitive and behavioral psychology, general semantics, linguistics, and other fields, about how our minds and bodies work.[4] One of their conclusions was that we were all capable of modeling and reproducing excellence. For a bibliography of resources on NLP see the links section of our Web site, www.successtechnologies.com.

They also realized that we each had our own preferred way of performing certain tasks. In essence, they concluded that by becoming aware of what you do, how you think, what you feel, and what you say to yourself when you are learning, applying knowledge, or teaching, you can become more proficient and effective in the performance of those tasks. You can begin to enjoy them more.

Furthermore, the creators of NLP felt that if one person is able to perform some task in an exceptional way, then it may be possible for others to re-create that excellence by learning that person's model. Many of the exercises throughout this book are designed to open your mind to knowledge you already possess but do not yet use as often as you might.

They are intended to allow you to discover, practice, and use your own models of excellence and to notice and reproduce the excellence of others. When you begin to experience life as a time of learning, a time of enjoyment, and a time of fulfillment, your children will begin to model your behavior and learn from everyone they meet. They will enjoy learning and make better judgments about what is useful and healthy for them. Remember, they're watching and listening to you. They really want to learn. You should make it an enjoyable experience for them![5]

The social learning theory articulated by the psychologist Albert Bandra, as well as common sense and our own experiences, all also suggest that our children learn by modeling our behaviors and beliefs. So set a great example. Become familiar with your own natural or learned methods of learning and developing your personal intelligence. Become familiar with the tools of great learners and thinkers. For example, in *Sparks of Genius*, Robert and Michele Root-Bernstein set out thirteen "think tools" of the world's most creative people. Seek out opportunities to become a better learner and bring your children of all ages along for the ride.

Quantum Learning Exercise

For now, remember that feeling better produces better results, and faster and more efficient learning. And when you feel great life can generally be more enjoyable and productive. Excellence is rarely the product of envy or a passionless life. The following exercise will help you to produce the results you desire.

Step #1: If possible find a quiet place and put on some music. Use music or background sounds which you find inspirational or interesting. Make it the sort of music or sound that you would enjoy listening to if you were studying, or that makes you feel like you are already learning. In some cases, you might feel best with a very quiet environment. In that case, find one or create one.

Step #2: On a separate piece of paper, or in your journal, write down five (5) times (specific times) when you remember that you were able to learn something quickly and easily. Or remember and note specific times when you had a breakthrough in learning where perhaps you felt confused but then suddenly you seemed to be clear and able to understand.

If you can't remember five specific times then use your imagination and make them up.

As you will see, the more you begin to remember and re-experience the times in your life when you learned quickly and easily or when you brought clarity from confusion, the more certain you become that you are able to do this, the more empowered you feel, and the more your unconscious mind begins to notice what was similar about all of these situations and how you actually go about learning. You do not need to be consciously aware of this in order for it to work. However, it is useful to do the exercise. It helps your unconscious mind to make connections. Sometimes our conscious mind will sort things out and make judgments on its own. That is okay. When we become consciously aware of how we do something we can choose to practice it. If you prefer, you can simply allow the unconscious mind to do the heavy lifting for you and begin to naturally and easily reproduce these optimal states of learning without consciously trying.

Conclusion

When you have something to learn, whether physical or factual, become aware that **you are learning** and focus on learning. Begin to do it in a way that is designed to be optimal for you. To do this, you must first become aware of how you learn and then make learning and using your new knowledge so enjoyable and seductive that you feel compelled to learn. Become aware of how efficient you already are and how learning enhances your life.

Reminders and Actions

- Remind yourself of specific times when you were a great learner.
- Become aware of how you learn and practice enjoying it even when it seems hard to do so.
- Remember to create the learning environment that is optimal for you.[6]
- Be aware that even difficult learning can be rewarding. Think of a time when learning seemed hard but the results were soooo good!
- Be a good learning role model for kids. Show them how you do it. Help to get them to be in the right mindset for optimal learning.
- Register at www.successtechnologies.com and e-mail a request for the Brain-Booster Bibliography. This is a list of great brain-boosting and creativity books as well as Web-based resources.

Chapter

2

Beliefs and Enhanced Communication

*"Why sometimes I have believed as many
as six impossible things before breakfast."*

—Lewis Carroll, *Alice in Wonderland*

An insight that surfaces for many people in reading Chapter One and doing the exercises is the realization that they have preexisting beliefs about learning, communication, and parenting which are highly beneficial or in some cases detrimental. Most parents, physicians, therapists, and businesspeople who are great communicators have similar beliefs that help to make them great communicators. Poor communicators, on the other hand, tend to report many disempowering beliefs. For example, in Chapter One I asked you to write down specific times when you remembered being confused about something and then broke through to clarity and understanding. Great learners believe that confusion leads to clarity. Many times, poor learners become discouraged by confusion. They believe that confusion is a barrier to learning and they give up just before the breakthrough.

Scientists who study learning (and many people who simply examine their experiences) have begun to realize that when you are learning new information, the process of learning requires you to examine that information, and often your world, in a different way. It also requires you to synthesize this information and combine it with what you already know. This process produces even more complex information and can result in periods of temporary confusion.[7] If you realize, as you gather information and examine things in a new way, that this "confusion" usually precedes insight and understanding then confusion is less aggravating. In fact, when you realize that confusion is good then the confusion will itself propel you toward the result you desire. When you view confusion as a barrier rather than as a powerful propulsion system, then you can give up too soon. Therefore, I ask you to adopt the belief that **"Confusion is a steppingstone that leads to clarity."**

Adopting New Beliefs
Belief: Confusion Leads to Clarity—Keep Going!

Recognizing your empowering and disempowering beliefs and how they are expressed and perpetuated in language is another tool of learning that will serve you well throughout this book and in your life.[8] For example, consider the belief

"I just don't learn well." That's not very useful. "I am already a natural learner." is an improvement, isn't it? As a belief it is pleasurable and far superior to the belief that "I just don't learn well." You see, beliefs are like filters or lenses. They alter your perceptions. When you hold a belief it helps you sort out or simplify the enormous and complex amount of data in the world. Therefore, if you believe that you are not a good learner you will become consciously aware of and notice evidence that supports that belief. However, if you believe that confusion leads to understanding and learning, and that you are already a good communicator just getting better and better, then you will begin to notice the things that make you aware of the truth of these more useful beliefs. All of this falls under the simple concept "You get what you look for."

You Get What You Look For

There are very good neurological and biological reasons for the statement "You get what you look for." Within each of our minds there is something known as the reticular activating system or RAS. The RAS is located in the portion of the brain known as the medulla. It is not so much a physical structure as it is a piece of software. The RAS conducts an unconscious search of the world for what we tell it to look for. For example, have you ever had the experience of purchasing a new car, dress or some other item and then you began to notice it everywhere? This is because the reticular activator has become aware of it and has activated an automatic search function. In the not-too-distant past, the RAS was essential to nutrition and to survival. Before the advent of supermarkets and fast food restaurants, each person, family, tribe or other social unit was responsible for obtaining its own food. The world was also a very dangerous place.

Hunters and gatherers would decide that they were looking for a particular type of food. Imagine for a moment that you are a gatherer looking for a berry. You decide you want a berry. As you move through your day, the RAS unconsciously scans all of the information you receive through your senses of sight, sound and smell and calls to your attention anything that indicates a berry. You become consciously aware of the berry. You can now decide if it is edible and if it is, you harvest it.

The RAS also looked constantly for evidence of danger. It was designed to keep you safe in a violent world. For that reason, the RAS tends to emphasize and exaggerate risk. In an effort to protect us, it often calls "danger" to our attention.

In modern times we often misuse our RAS. We give it bad suggestions. Remember, the RAS has a tendency to exaggerate risk for our own good. Yet we seem surprised when it calls unpleasant matters to our attention. For example, I've had seminar participants tell me that when their alarm clocks go off it is not uncommon for them to shut off the alarm and before they even get up they think to themselves "How could today possibly be worse than yesterday?" This is, in essence, a search command to the RAS. Alarm bells go off in the mind and the brain's software begins to tell it to look for any evidence that today is going to be worse than yesterday. The RAS exaggerates the danger to be sure that you become aware. These are the things you begin to notice.

You become aware of them and then you say things to yourself to confirm that you are indeed having a bad day. It is a cycle that creates a self-fulfilling prophecy.

So you can see that giving our unconscious mind and the RAS commands that help us to search for what we actually want is vastly superior to asking them to help us search for unpleasantries. Who will be the more inspiring, interesting, and enjoyable parent: the parent focused on failure—their own or a child's—or the parent who is searching for vitality and success in life?

"You Get What You Look For" Exercise

Let us consider another proof of how we use the RAS. As you sit there, look around you and *notice everything around you that is* **red**. Do you notice anything red? Now without looking try to remember everything that is…..

green.

Don't look! Did you have to look? You probably didn't notice anything green because you weren't looking for it! You were looking for red. Understanding this aspect of our minds is incredibly important. Why? Because we get what we look for. Remember to ask yourself and your kids the type of questions that get them looking for the good stuff in life. More on how to use this with your kids later. For now, practice using this knowledge on yourself.

When you catch yourself asking unproductive questions just change! At night and in the morning get into the habit of asking more interesting questions. Make it habitual. Pick one or make up your own: How is today going to be even better than yesterday? What can I do to feel better today? How can I help someone else today? How can I feel ecstatic today?

Sounds are also useful in this context. Each day, as soon as I wake up, I say to myself "Ooooooooooooooooh yeah! This feels good." Some days I actually say it out loud! It is impossible to say "Oooooooooooh yeah! This feels good" and not feel better. Your brain hears those sounds and knows that whenever it hears those sounds that good experiences are occurring or are soon to occur. It produces electrochemical reactions throughout the body. Powerful neurotransmitters are released. It puts us in a desirable physical state. From this desirable state we can ask more empowering questions about our day and there are good scientific reasons to believe that we will in fact get what we look for—a radically better day. Who will be the more effective parent— the parent who is depressed, angry and anxious or the parent whose mind, body, and language all tell a child that life is a gift to be enjoyed?

If you get what you look for you should look for the good, great, and awesome things. So there are several beliefs that I would like you to adopt, if only temporarily, but certainly while you are reading this book and experimenting with the techniques that could benefit you. You do not actually have to adopt them. Just pretend. Play along for now and act "as if" you already have adopted them. Then you be the judge. These beliefs often become the basis for radically better use of the RAS.

Adopt These Beliefs

Act "as if" you *already* have these beliefs:

1. I am already an effective communicator in certain circumstances.
2. I can expand my effectiveness.
3. I learn quickly and easily.
4. Confusion precedes understanding, certainty, and creativity.
5. I can enjoy this book and the process of using the information.
6. The quality of my communication is the quality of the response I get.[9]

If you adopt these beliefs, or fervently pretend to hold them, and act as if you believe them, your unconscious mind is going to begin to perform different tasks. It will begin to filter information in a new and more useful way. You will begin to experience the evidence to support these beliefs. Later you can decide whether or not you like the beliefs and whether or not you want to keep them.

Conclusion

You learn faster and more efficiently when you remember and re-experience times in your life when you were a great learner. When you do this, the brain releases powerful neurotransmitters that were released at the time of the original event and the body and mind become more vital.[10] You are a better communicator when you remember times when you were already effective. This is because you have a way of learning or communicating that is most effective for you and because your mind and body re-create the experience of effective communication. Can you learn to learn or communicate even more efficiently? Yes! You simply need to adopt the beliefs that great learners and communicators already use. You need to notice any area of your life where you learn faster and better and begin to use those rules and methods when learning in other areas. You also need to notice how others learn. Ask better questions and above all enjoy this book and the learning process. Your satisfaction and your child's desire to learn depend upon you.

Reminders and Actions

- Beliefs are filters that help you to simplify a very complex world. However, they alter your experience of the world and what you look for. Experiment and pick your own *enhanced* beliefs about parenting, communication with your children, and learning. For example "I feel overwhelmed by the demands on me" becomes "Each day I feel more skilled at dealing with the demands on me as a parent" or "I'm excited to discover better parenting skills all the time."

- Adopt, or pretend to adopt, the major beliefs and strategies utilized by great communicators before studying the tactics.

- You may find that just pretending to adopt those beliefs results in substantial improvement. Remember, you get what you look for. You can look around all day long for evidence that you are not good at communicating as a parent. Or, you can begin *now* to notice what you do well and how you can do it better.

- Adopt the belief (if only for purposes of experimentation

and for as long as it serves you well) that "**The quality of my communication is the quality of the response I get.**" This puts some responsibility on you and it is harder to say that the reason people didn't do what you wanted is because they were just dumb.

- A change in physiology changes your mindset. Put your body in a great physiology (let yourself feel good) and a great mindset often results. Specifically, sit or stand the way you do when **you feel great**. Breathe, hold your head and shoulders the way that you do when you feel strong and remember a time when you communicated effectively.

- Model these beliefs so that children can learn by mimicking you.

Part Two

The Strategies of Great Communicators

"Thus, what concerns us here is not imagination in itself, but rather creative imagination and the faculty that helps us pass from the level of conception to the level of realization."

—Composer Igor Stravinsky

Introduction to
Part Two

When we view our role as parents and great family communicators as an expedition or undertaking worthy of practice and planning it becomes more exciting and engaging. We think about it more often and we also come to realize that the knowledge used by great communicators (which is essential to great family relationships) can be broken down into two broad categories. The first category includes the principles or strategies of communication. The second category is comprised of the tactics of communications.

Strategies are the big-picture issues. They are the principles, ideas, mindsets, and knowledge that underlie all effective communication and parenting skills. The tactics are the particular tools we use to achieve our strategic goals. Strategies are the large objectives and skills that help us to achieve each of our goals and which guide the use of the tactics or the tools in the toolbox.

In this section we will review the big concepts of successful communication that guide our choice and use of techniques. When you understand the big issues, when you adopt the mindset of great communication, then the techniques fall into place.

3

Know Your Desired Result and Have a Plan—The First Strategy of Success

"Chance favors the prepared mind."

—Scientist Louis Pasteur

J ust as every person has an optimal learning strategy, every successful person also has a process or system that produces success. It's the way they go about achieving what they desire. It's their plan. If you ask successful people how they do it, they will give you a variety of answers. If you ask successful parents and communicators to describe their process, they tell you what they *consciously* know about how they "did it." They will describe to you many of the ways by which they *think* they got good results. However, our processes are usually not in our conscious awareness. Think about it. The better you get at something, the less frequently you think about how you do it once you learn it well. The process becomes unconscious. Think about driving a car. The process of driving a car, once we learn it well, is outside of our ordinary awareness. However, if we really understand a process we can reproduce it, improve it, and use it more often.

You are reading a book about language and parenting and communication. Why did you buy it? Why are you reading it? How can this book improve your life? What will you or your family gain? You need to be clear about what you desire so that you maximize the benefits as you read. So for the next few minutes we will examine success and the formula for achieving it.

Just as when you communicate with children, you need to be clear with yourself about what you desire. If you are confused (or unclear) you are less likely to get it.

Clarify What You Mean by Success

Let's examine two underlying concepts for clarity. The first is success. What is it? And how will we know when we have it? When we talk about successful people, we are usually talking about success in a variety of areas: financial, artistic, spiritual, and of course parenting successes. Furthermore, there is no one definition of success in any of these areas. We all define success differently, and we define success in different areas of our lives differently. You may feel that you are successful at your job because you make money, and enjoy it. However, making money is not usually one of the criteria when judging our family or spiritual lives. There are different criteria for defining success in parenting. There may be certain qualities that we can agree constitute success in communication as a parent and which we believe make us successful parents. In parenting, for example, we want children who are well-adjusted, who are good problem solvers, who are kind without losing self-esteem. For you there may be other criteria, too. What does success mean to you in this context?

The next question is how will you know when you are successful as a parent? What will you see? How will you feel? Only when you know this can you really begin to move in the direction of your success. Fortunately, there is a way to discover what you want and how to move in that direction.

Follow the Plan of Success

If we observe the behaviors of successful people rather than listening solely to their descriptions of success, a very clear pattern emerges. They all follow a very basic yet powerful process. Many have described this process. The number of steps varies depending on how you group certain tasks. However, a simple and elegant strategy for success in just about any endeavor is to:

1. Know your desired result.
2. Develop a plan to achieve it.
3. Take action!
4. Develop flexibility and your sensory acuity.
5. When you reach your goal, celebrate your success and set new goals.

Your own way of achieving may vary slightly in its syntax or execution, but if you take a moment now to examine a specific area of your life and specific times when you were successful in it, you are likely to find all of these elements. So that you can become aware of how you've done it in the past, and enhance your future success, let's break down the system and examine each part of the success formula and how to make it work best for you.

1. Know Your Desired Result

This has variously been described as "know what you want," "be careful what you wish for," and "be sure to set clear goals." For me, "Know the result or outcome you desire," is a great way to say it. In essence, this means you must clarify what you desire. Now this sounds easy but people who are successful do this step in a very different way. In their minds, they really experience the desired result. They see it, feel it, watch it, and experience it. They imagine it vividly (but in many cases unconsciously). They ask themselves what it would be like if they had this outcome. How would they feel? What specific benefits would they experience? How would it benefit others? What would they gain and what would they lose?

In this way, they refine their desire. The desire is no longer an oblique general goal. Often, when I am working with people on this phase of the success plan they say things like "I want more money," "I want my kids to be more polite," or "I want to be a better communicator." These goals lack clarity, detail, and motivating force. They are so vague you might not even realize it if you achieved them.

However, when you imagine not only what it is you want but exactly how your life would be different, what would improve, and how would you act if you already had it, then you have information that compels you to act. This means that when you establish the result you want with respect to family communication you have to make the desires clear *and* motivational. They have to be so desirable, so attractive to you that you will *consistently* allocate time and energy to achieving these outcomes. When you love your work, your success is much more likely, if not assured. Likewise, if your goals are truly compelling you will love working toward them. Your goals will *pull* you toward them.

So let's begin with your imagination. Ideally, you should write down at least five desired outcomes that you'll get from reading this book. Surprisingly, your mother (if she ever said this) was right again. Remember, I said earlier that you actually do get what you look for. Again, there is a biological basis for this natural law. It is called the reticular activating system or RAS. This, as you recall, is a part of the brain which, among other things, helps your unconscious mind to search for things that you have decided you want or need. If you ask, "Why don't my children do what I ask them?" the RAS gets to work looking for the answer. This answer is usually not very exciting or motivating. The answer to that question is usually dark. It is usually not true but you have asked for the answer. Your mind does not want to disappoint you. It makes stuff up.

But when you design and write down a set of outcomes that you truly and passionately desire, you activate the RAS in more positive ways. We are motivated to keep going when we ask: "How can I make this more exciting? How can I engage my son's or daughter's imagination? How can I do this in a way that makes me feel awesome, excited, delighted?" Now let us begin with an exercise.

You Get What You Look For—Using Your Power for Good, Not Evil

What five results do I desire from reading this book?

For example you might want to stimulate a child to do better in school or to listen to you more attentively. You might want to avoid arguments but still be an effective and concerned parent. If your child is an adult you might want them to consider your opinions or seek you out more often. On a sheet of paper write down five results that you desire from this book. For a variety of reasons, all scientifically well established, it is important to actually write them down. Remember that retention soars when you or your kids use multiple modalities of processing information.

Now take a moment and rank these desired outcomes according to priority. In other words, rank the one that would create the most dramatic and powerful improvement for you, the one that would most radically improve your life as number one. Then rank as number two the next most desired outcome, etcetera.

Whenever you take the opportunity to think about your life it is important to take the next step. In other words, you have only so much time and energy. You can, or will, make only so many changes to improve your life. So, once you have clarified your desired outcomes then think about which ones will generate the most positive results. Begin by applying your energy to these areas.

Balance Is the Best

Now let me ask you something. If you had radical improvement in one or two areas of your life but you ignored all of the others what would happen? Would your life be out of balance? Would that be good? If you became a better communicator at home but ignored work would your life improve radically? If you became spiritually stronger but neglected exercise would you remain healthy?

So you need to ask yourself some more good questions. What areas of my life are most important to my overall well-being? What would I have to do to improve in all of these areas? How could I enjoy all of this improvement? How would my life be better? What would I gain? What would I lose? Can I enjoy these improvements so much that I do not mind losing what I might lose?

2. Develop a Plan

When you develop a plan you need to remember and believe that **it is *not* necessary that everything go as planned**. For example, there is no one more fascinated by, and more constantly involved in, the process of planning than our business and military leaders. However, no one, except parents, faces more variables than our business leaders and our military leaders. Rarely, in fact, do things go as they planned.

You may then ask, "What is the point of all the planning? Why do these leaders spend inordinate amounts of time and money developing plans if they are rarely utilized?" The answer is that the plans are usually utilized but things just do not always go according to the plan. The plan itself, however, gives you confidence to act. You have examined the options, their possible outcomes, the resources available to you and other factors. Planning gives you the *confidence to proceed without fear*. You want to go into the lifelong process of having great family relationships with confidence. Planning also helps us to be more organized. We know what we'll need and what to do. It makes taking action easier and more efficient.

Planning begins with identifying the result you desire, the resources you have available, additional resources you might need, and determining how to get them. The plan then suggests the method for bringing these factors together in the way that will most elegantly and easily achieve your desired outcome. You know, from your list, what your desired outcome is in each of these areas.

Resources

The next step is to identify the resources you already have. In this way we come at a task from a position of strength and motivation rather than from fear and wondering what it is that we lack. It is important to sit down and spend a few moments identifying all of the resources you have available to achieve your desired outcomes. You may be surprised by how many resources you have. For example, if one of your desired outcomes is more time with your children, spouse, or others, what resources could help with this?

Do you have a supportive spouse or partner? Do you have family members who would spend time with the children so that you can spend time alone with your spouse? Do you have financial resources that would allow you to take a vacation or engage in an activity or class with your children? It is important to *list as many as possible*. Do not evaluate the list at this time. Anything that leaps to mind, write it down, no matter how silly it may seem. You may be surprised later to find that some of the things you wrote down as resources, which at first seemed silly, can end up being just the ticket to solve your problem or give you your result.

Next, you need to identify resources that you may need but do not yet have. Do you need help? How will you get it? A great way to discover resources is to imagine that you already have the result and work back in time. How did you get there? What did you need? How did you get those things?

3. Take Action

Of the small percentage of people who actually engage in the process we have already reviewed, very few of them ever take action. People just do not implement their plans. Of those who do, many haven't prioritized and consequently, they feel overwhelmed and stop before reaching their goal. This is why you want to start from a point that is so powerful and motivating you feel compelled to keep moving toward your goal. You need to build motivation into your plan from the start. You need to recognize that you may begin, from time to time, to lose momentum. Know the warning signs and be prepared to make yourself keep going.

How do you stay motivated? Begin by choosing goals and outcomes which are themselves so compelling that they are irresistible. They seduce you. That is easy when it comes to kids. How would your life and your children's lives improve if you became a better communicator? How would they look, act, and feel; what could they achieve? On the other hand, what if you do not improve? What if you just keep doing things the same old way? Will their lives improve? How will they be harmed?

You can see from these questions that you do have a choice of doing something to improve your own life and their lives or staying the same, making the same mistakes, possibly harming your children and later your grandchildren. Which do you choose? How compelling is that?

4. Develop Flexibility and Your Sensory Acuity

To be truly successful in developing great communication skills, it is essential to develop a sense of flexibility and the skills of sensory acuity. There is a saying that the most flexible part of any system usually controls the system. For that reason, we want to become more skilled at observing, listening, and judging whether or not our plan is working. When it is not working we want to enjoy the process of revising our plans. In communication, what worked last week may not work today. What worked this morning may not work this afternoon. We need flexibility. This comes through to children young and old alike. They will know if we are becoming increasingly frustrated or if we are relaxed. So how do we do this? Aren't we either flexible or not from birth?

The truth is that flexibility of behavior and the mind is like flexibility of the body. Only with practice and gentle stretching does it develop. I have some personal experience in this regard. I am a second dan black belt and a certified martial arts instructor. At the age of thirty-two I took up the martial arts to spend time with my oldest son and a short time later with my daughter. At thirty-two my body was inflexible.

A "split" had something to do with ice cream—it wasn't something I did with my legs. However, at the gym I saw grandmothers and grandfathers doing full splits and graceful stretches. When I first tried a split I confronted a new reality—I was inflexible. Now I could have stopped there and remained inflexible. Instead, I decided to **become more flexible**. I started stretching. I asked new questions. How do you breathe? How far do you go? Sometimes I would rush and pull a muscle. Eventually, I became more flexible. I could move more smoothly.

Behavior is like that. **Practice feeling good for no reason at all**. If you can feel good for no reason at all then you can feel good for any reason. When will you make better decisions, when you feel great or when you are despondent? Feel better through practicing. When you feel good you make better decisions, you're more confident and flexible. This makes you a better communicator. Kids of any age will find you a more wonderful parent when you are flexible enough to understand their thoughts, fears, and desires. It is not necessary to agree but it is better to be flexible enough to understand.

Now a word about sensory acuity. Practice watching and listening. You may be surprised how much you can learn through a moment of silence. When you are better at observing and listening you will know if your plan is working. You will be respectful of others' views. You will allow your children to work out their own solutions. Often the best communicators simply give others the chance to work out their own problems. Researchers examining male/female dating have observed that men who primarily listen are perceived by their dates as being "very interesting" and "highly engaging." Men who speak more are less favorably rated.

5. When You Reach Your Goal, Celebrate Your Success and Set New Goals

Make goal setting and achievement a habit. When you are aware that you have achieved a goal or even progressed toward it, celebrate your achievement. Reward yourself. Make the achievement of goals exciting.[11] Make a habit of enjoying your success. Then move on and ask new questions. You are now an improved you. You are now capable of asking even more informed, thoughtful, and useful questions. How can you improve even more? Are there other ways that you and your family can benefit? Apply the techniques and search out new resources.

Notice that this process does not end here. It is a cycle. The final step in the process sends us back to the beginning. We have new goals and start all over. However, when we return to step one there is a new, more flexible, creative, and powerful mind at work. Each time we go through the process it improves us. Once improved, our new mind goes to work on even better solutions. It is an upward spiral of improvement.

Conclusion

In any task you undertake it is important to clearly envision the outcome you desire. You should be able to see it, feel it, and understand what it would be like to experience and have it. Make your desired outcomes and your goals so exciting that they motivate you and compel you to act. You should have a plan of action with respect to this book. What would you like to get out of it? How would you like your communication with your family, your spouse, and your friends to be different? How could these changes radically improve your life? Remember that the strategies described in this chapter are those utilized by successful people throughout time and in many walks of life to achieve their success.

Reminders and Actions

- Develop a plan for getting results from this book.
- Decide what you would like to achieve and determine exactly how your life would be radically better if you achieved it.
- Be aware of your actions and whether they are leading you closer to your goals or further away. **Be willing to adapt your plan.**
- Go to www.successtechnologies.com to get the Brain-Booster Bibliography, to register for newsletters or updates, and download a free communications wallet card. If you are not a computer person, send a self-addressed, stamped envelope to Success Technologies, Inc., P. O. Box 507, Malvern, Pennsylvania 19355 and ask for a wallet card.
- Anthony Robbins is one of today's most sought-after speakers and consultants. His *Time of Your Life*—Time Management System and goal-setting products are very powerful and can be ordered at www.tonyrobbins.com.

Chapter

4

Speak and Act
Congruently

*"We have too many high-sounding words, and
too few actions that correspond with them."*
—Co-founder of modern democracy Abigail Adams,
in a letter to John Adams, 1774

Have you ever met a family that seems really well
adjusted? The kids seem to listen. The parents seem
so calm. What characteristics do you admire most?
Which of these qualities would you like to have more of?

There are such families. Do they have discord? Do they
have problems? Do they shout at one another? Yes, from
time to time they probably do all of those things. However,
their success is not just an illusion. I come from a family like
that and I have a family like that. When I was growing up
we had plenty of problems and daily challenges. And yet,
there was a level of respect and a level of success in commu-

nication that made life enjoyable. Where did that come from? My parents got married when they were 18. They had three children by the time they were 21. They were not formally educated at a university level. But at 61 they are still married, they are financially successful, and they have relationships with all of their children and grandchildren. They have pretty good communication and problem solving skills. As children we acquired those skills by modeling our parents, other adults, and teachers. What are the skills employed by great parents and great communicators? One of the primary ones is congruency in communication.

Great Communicators Act Congruently

As parents, one of the best things we can do for our children is to speak and act congruently so that they can model our successful behaviors. This is not just a matter of "Do as I say, not as I do." Congruency means more than that. It means being sure that our words, tone of voice, body language, gestures, and actions are in agreement, not conflict. When we are certain, when we trust our gut, and when we are congruent, our communication is efficient, easy, and effective. It may even become enjoyable. Dr. Peter Goldenthal, author of *Beyond Sibling Rivalry*, speaks of this when he says that the best sort of parent/child communication comes "from the soul." It is communication that the parent and child experience at the deepest level.

Congruency is one of the most important rules of communication. It is important when dealing with anyone but it is particularly important when you are communicating with or teaching children. Let me remind you of how powerful this can be.

Have you ever had the experience of asking a question and receiving the answer you were hoping for but you knew, by the way the person said it, that it wouldn't work? You knew that you wouldn't get what you were looking for? That is because the answer you received was not delivered in a congruent way. The person may have said "yes" while shaking their head no. They may have said "great!" while appearing or sounding disinterested.

When we communicate with one another, we pay attention to every aspect of our communication. When we are face to face, we quickly assess a speaker's posture, tone of voice, body motions, pace of speech, breathing, and many other factors. In fact, when there is a doubt about meaning, a conflict between the words being used and those other factors, we will tend to believe the other factors and actually ignore the words. At the very least, when such conflicts occur we will feel uncomfortable. We will sense doubt. Children are adept at ferreting out these incongruencies. They pay *more* attention to how we are saying something than what we are saying. In fact, adults do the same thing.

Obviously, we do not want children or adults to feel doubt or uncertainty when we talk to them. We want them to believe us. We want to be credible. We want them to feel that they can trust us. This requires thought—and congruency. Am I right about this?

Most people believe that it is the language (the words) they select which transmits most of the meaning. Many scientific studies have been conducted which confirmed that in face-to-face communication, the words we select make up a very small percentage of the overall communication.[12] In fact, some studies have indicated that as little as 7% of communication is contained in the selection of vocabulary. What makes up the rest? Things like the tone of our voice, the speed of our speech, the pace of our breathing, any gestures we make, even our posture (are we leaning forward, nodding?). These are some of the factors we observe in others when they speak to us. If we are paying attention only to the *words* we use we may be ignoring some of the most important stuff. We are ignoring some things that really matter.

For example, do the words "Beautiful!" and "Right!" have the same meaning when they are delivered with an angry or sarcastic tone of voice as they do when spoken by a proud or delighted parent or spouse? No. They have the opposite meaning. Which meaning does the recipient pay attention to? The meaning contained in the tone of voice, coupled perhaps with an angry posture, is what controls. It is not the words. We can actually harm children with our tone of voice even if we say the right words. We can tell them we are bored even if we're parroting words that say we are engaged. If we want to become master communicators we have to become aware of the signals we're sending in ways other than the words we choose. Our voice tone, the speed of our speech, breathing, and posture say more than the words. When those factors match the words, there is no ambiguity. The receiver knows more precisely what we mean.

Think about the speed of your voice. If you want to convey excitement do you speak in a low, slow, monotone? If you want to calm down a situation do you keep speaking quickly or even frantically? Become aware of the message contained in the speed of your speech. Likewise, be ware of your gestures. If a parent says "I am proud of you" but turns away or has a "closed" body posture (such as crossed arms) the praise may be less effective than the same words stated directly to the child with good eye contact and an "open" posture. Angry gestures or words hissed through clenched teeth can overpower the most carefully chosen words. Of course, these are extreme examples to get you thinking.

We need to pay more attention to how our words and other factors affect the person we are talking to. For the rest of this book and for the rest of your life, you should consider adopting the following belief: THE QUALITY OF MY COMMUNICATION IS THE QUALITY OF THE RESPONSE I GET.[13]

When you accept this, you begin to take responsibility for your communication. That belief requires that you become more aware that there are other factors such as congruency that are vitally important. It requires you to become aware that people process the words we say in radically different ways. Therefore, we must check to see if we're being understood. When a child or spouse fails to understand us, it's easy to say to ourselves, "He didn't pay attention," or "She never does what I tell her." However, blaming like this fails to get us what we want. It creates resentment and makes future failures more likely, not less.

Conclusion

Actions speak louder than words. In order to be persuasive, trusted, and believed by our children we need to be congruent in our communication. We cannot give voice to one idea while our behaviors suggest that it is unimportant or wrong. Be careful to speak congruently. Your actions, words, gestures, and body language should all match. Be aware of this.

Reminders and Actions

- Practice speaking and acting congruently.
- Become aware of your voice qualities—use the right voice.
- Become aware of tonality—use appropriate tones of voice.
- Become aware of speed—speak at the appropriate rate of speed.
- Become aware of gestures—use gestures that match or emphasize your message.
- Become aware of body language—your body language should complement your message.
- Become aware of how others are reacting to these factors. You may think your tone of voice is great. A child may think otherwise. Do you care? Then observe their reactions.
- Adopt the belief that the quality of your communication is the quality of the response you get.

  NOTE: I found it very interesting, that my editor asked me if we can really "choose" the right tone of voice. She made the savvy observation that if we choose it consciously and it conflicts with our feelings, then it might seem contrived. She's right. If we're *mad* and we "fake" a sweet tone of voice it will seem incongruent (the very thing that we don't want).

That's where behavioral flexibility comes in. We *can* learn to stop. We can realize that there is a gap between cause and effect. Then, we can sometimes avoid "snapping" when we're mad. We can make our emotions *and* our words, tone of voice, and body language all match in a way to achieve our desired result.

5

The Limits of Language— Avoiding Confusion

"I understand a fury in your words, but not the words."

—William Shakespeare, *Othello*

I said earlier that when our communication fails we often blame the other party. How many times have you said to yourself "He just never listens to me?" That is not a very useful belief. What if instead you chose to say, "That didn't work this time?" What if you asked yourself, "How might I be clearer, more precise, and more persuasive?" Remember that even when you are congruent in your communication, language still has its limitations. Language is full of noise or interference because we all believe that words mean the same thing to everyone else as they do to us. But everyone processes information and words in different ways. And most words have multiple meanings anyway. For example, if I say "I like fish," what do I mean? Does that sentence mean that I like to see them swim? And if that is what it means do I like them in an aquarium or in nature? It also might mean that I like to eat them-I like their flavor. It could mean any of those things. How do we avoid this linguistic confusion? We can radically improve our communication by examining this concept of noise, or "communication distortion," in more detail.[14]

If you say to your spouse or partner, "I would like a turkey sandwich," have you really asked them to get you one? No. You have simply made an observation. Maybe they should "get it" but that doesn't necessarily get you to where you want to be. What if, instead, you said, "I am hungry and I am working on this project. Would you please get me a turkey sandwich?" That's better. You've actually told them more. You've said you're hungry so you hope they understand that you want the sandwich now. You have asked for it. But you haven't really asked for what you want. You are still keeping some of your desires a secret. And you haven't given them a good reason to help you. So far, there is nothing in the request for them.

Let's do one better. "I'm busy doing this for the children. I would love it if you could get me a turkey sandwich *right now*. Will you?" Now you have laid the groundwork. You've asked for a response within a certain time frame, explained that you are doing something for the children (something of mutual interest) and apparently asked for what you want. This is much better communication. However, the "requesting spouse" in this example has still fallen into the trap of believing that the "receiving spouse" gets the same meaning from the words "turkey sandwich."

When I say "turkey sandwich" to you what do you think of, see, or experience? When I ask for a turkey sandwich I want the meat shaved, the bread to be rye (or in a pinch whole wheat) with very little mayo and sometimes (but only *sometimes*) a slice of cheddar. Was your picture or experience of a "turkey sandwich" different from mine in any way? Were there numerous differences in how you interpreted the words "turkey sandwich"? What were the differences? Was your turkey thin or thick? Was your bread rye, whole wheat, or white or, maybe even a kaiser roll? Were you enjoying the sandwich when you heard the words or did you just see it? Did you taste or smell it? Did yours have mayo, cheese, or tomato? Salt and pepper?

Have you ever asked your spouse or partner or a child for something and gotten something you were not expecting? Maybe it didn't even resemble what you wanted. This is usually the reason: The quality of your request may have been less than optimal yet you assumed the meaning was clear. Now I know that many of us feel that it's our spouse's, partner's or child's responsibility to know our needs or to love us enough to find them out. However, if we help them, we may discover that they love getting it right.

There is a tendency to believe that our own internal experience of words is the same as our spouse's or our children's.

If we believe that the quality of our communication is the quality of the response we get, we will make sure that the recipient of our request understands it. Of course, this can be done in a patronizing tone of voice (almost certain to fail when used with spouses and children) or a truly loving and appreciative tone of voice. You get to choose. Which will result in greater happiness and harmony?

Obvious, you say? Check throughout the day to see how often you violate these simple ideas. And now that you are aware, begin to notice how often you take the time to be sure that you are understood. Which way gets better results? Which way is more fun?

This is also a two-way street. Remember, when someone asks you for a turkey sandwich, your tendency is to assume that they want the turkey sandwich in your mind. Stop. Ask them what they really want. They will appreciate it. They may even love you for the concern you are showing.

Having said that words are not clear, it does not follow that words are unimportant. Words do matter and they matter very much to children. Be careful in selecting your words—especially when angry. Make it a practice to pause in that situation and carefully consider your choice. Words do matter and the meaning to your child matters. Something that rarely occurs to parents is to discover what words mean to your children. However, if you ask them they will tell you. If you ask a child, even a young child "What must a mother do to be a great mother?", they will tell you. If you ask "How do you know that I love you?", they will tell you.

You can ask children of all ages—directly or indirectly what words mean. They will tell you and you will know how to speak their language.

Conclusion

Do not just assume that the words you use have the same meaning to other people. You need to clarify what you are trying to say—first to yourself and then to others. Remember that when you make a request your voice tone and speed and gestures may further confuse your meaning if they do not agree. Be sure to check in a polite way to determine if you have been clear. And remember, clarity and congruency alone may not be motivating. Why should the person you are speaking to act? Remember to think of them. If words mean different things to different people, if they are open to various interpretations, then you must check to see if your meaning has been understood. You also need to check to see if you are understanding. Finally, words do matter. Pause to reflect on your choice of words—especially when you are angry.

Reminders and Actions

Continue to develop the skills you have learned so far:

- Know the result you want—if you are clear you'll be more likely to convey your needs and to receive what you desire.
- Be congruent in your request. Make your words, voice tones, gestures, body language, breathing, and eye contact all match the message.
- Adopt the beliefs that advance your goal of being a better

communicator. For example, "The quality of my communication is the quality of the results I get." If you don't get what you had in mind then you probably were not clear.

- Realize the limitations of language and check to see if you are being understood.
- Realize the limitations of language and check to see if you are understanding the other person.
- Have fun and be flexible. If something doesn't work the first time it only failed with that person and that time. It may work exquisitely the next time or with someone else. Be open-minded about success.
- Visit www.general-semantics.org for additional lessons in semantics and www.successtechnologies.com to register for newsletters or to receive a free communications wallet card.

Chapter

6

The Beauty of Silence, Time, and Listening

"I have found that the best way to give advice to your children is to find out what they want *and then advise them to do it."* (emphasis added)

—Harry Truman, president of the United States

No review of communication skills would be complete without an examination of the value of silence and the art of listening. Silence allows us an opportunity to hear our children, to watch them grow, and to love and experience them for who they really are. Silence and listening allow our children to work through their own problems, exercise their own creative genius, and to realize that we respect them. Of course, as parents we have a sacred obligation to see to the well-being of our children and help to guide them to appropriate and morally correct conclusions. Silence and listening do not equate with ignoring a bad judgment or idea.

However, if it is the parent who always guides the child, the child never comes to exercise their own skills of navigating through the world and of making sound decisions. He never gets to show his emotions or express his creativity. For that reason, it is important, from the time a child is young, to give the child ample opportunity to share his or her thoughts and to practice age-appropriate decision making. This can be done only through a combination of guidance, listening, and periods of silence and of letting go. We must overcome our culture's bias toward instructing children and learn to listen to our children. In this way, they come to trust us *and* themselves.[15]

One of the most effective ways of teaching children to move through the world, to exercise their imaginations, and to reach good conclusions is to make that a practice of our own. When we conduct ourselves in a particular way it is useful to call that to the child's attention. If we are successful, they will observe it. If we make a mistake it is okay to admit it, explore why we made the mistake, and describe what we have learned.[16]

For example, if a child has behaved inappropriately and you, as a parent, have overreacted it is not only acceptable but desirable to tell the child "I overreacted. If I had taken more time I might have responded in another way." The child appreciates that they have not been wronged by the parent and the parent has demonstrated that while they are not infallible, they love and care for the child and would seek to conduct themselves differently. However, the description should not end there. The parent might go on to ask in an age-appropriate way, "How would you respond or how else might you calm yourself if you were angry?" At this point, silence is appropriate. When we listen carefully to the child's response we can learn a lot. When we subject ourselves to this standard of behavior we are entitled to expect it from our children. If a teenage child overreacts, we can remind them of our own overreaction and how we learned from that.

Likewise, when a child expresses a problem it is our ordinary and understandable desire as parents to instruct and to offer a number of solutions. Instead, simple statements or questions followed by silence can be much more valuable to young, teenage, and adult children alike. When a child describes a problem consider saying "I see," "Tell me more," or "Why do you think that?" followed by silence. All of these responses offer the child the opportunity to further explore their own thinking, explain their thoughts, and make decisions. As children mature, we need to give them more opportunity to exercise independent thinking. However, if we wait until they are teenagers this faculty will be underdeveloped. Watch for opportunities to allow even young children to consider solutions of their own.

When a period of silence is followed by a child describing multiple possible outcomes, questions about how they will decide can again be helpful. "How will you decide which solution to use?" or "Which solution seems best to you now?" encourage the child to engage in the decision-making process. Again, by allowing the child to offer explanations to us we show respect for the child's own thinking processes. We help them to make thinking and decision making a habit and it gives us the opportunity to help guide that process when appropriate.

I am by no means suggesting that children will always arrive at appropriate conclusions. However, by allowing them to go through the process you will more clearly understand how the child is thinking, what they are thinking, and what factors they are considering. You will be in a much better position to guide their decision-making if your guidance is needed and you may be surprised and delighted to find that it is not often needed.

By regularly practicing the art of listening you will discover things about your children that might otherwise go unnoticed. When a child describes a problem and you suggest multiple solutions you are teaching the child to pick from solutions created by another person. This could create an unnecessary dependence on others. When you allow periods of silence and encourage a child's own internal processing instead, they begin to become more self-reliant and healthy children and later adults. Careful listening also reveals information about how the child thinks and processes language, and how they make decisions. Listening may reveal their true likes, dislikes, and pleasures. When you know how your child thinks and what gives them joy, your parenting and communication skills will surpass your expectations. These concepts will be explored more fully in the tactics chapters of Part Three and also in Chapter Eight.

When employing the art of silence and listening, consider modeling great listeners. Merely being silent and appearing to pay attention is not enough. Great listeners allow sufficient time and opportunity. Dr. Peter Goldenthal, author of *Beyond Sibling Rivalry*, reminded me in a recent interview that there is a significant time-to-disclosure ratio. Most children need time to begin to disclose their most important concerns. As children get older, it is especially true that they do not immediately begin to share their innermost thoughts, desires, and concerns. They need time.

Furthermore, you can be silent and yet not hear a thing your child says. Remember that there are many types of listening. One type of listening is focused listening. You are paying close attention. You are concentrating on the specific words and their meanings. Even then you can, of course, be focused on your own internal dialogue and ignore the person you are with. You need to focus and to be aware of your focus. Great listeners practice being aware of their focus. Is it internal or external? Is their listening focused on a particular person or is it generalized—i.e., listening to all of the sounds in the room?

As parents we must also remember that when we listen, we process the words in our own way. Some of us make pictures of the words. Some of us see the words themselves. Others create feelings in our bodies associated with the words. Remember, the words may also have different meanings to the speaker. Listen and question when you are uncertain of your child's meaning. In other words, listen like a young child. Become fascinated with communication.

All types of listening have their place. Effective listeners are simply aware of what they are doing and are able to shift their attention. Ideally, when we listen to our children we want to be keenly focused on them. Give your child your full attention. If another child interrupts it may be appropriate to say you are listening to the first child. In a moment, you might say, you can fully focus on them. Remember, in communication words are important but they make up perhaps as little as 7% of the message. Be aware of and pay attention to the other factors. Remember to "listen with your eyes, your ears and your body."

How do our children know we are listening? Great listeners usually signal their attentiveness through gestures, such as by tilting their heads slightly. They may say that they are listening and they make periodic eye contact. Direct and constant eye contact, however, tends to distract both the speaker *and* the listener. Learn to use your peripheral vision when listening.

Finally, remember to allow sufficient time. One way to do this is to make listening and time together a ritual. It could be that you listen to a story at each meal. You drive a child to school, or have a regular Saturday or Sunday time together. Making a special or quiet time for each child can also yield big returns—privacy matters. Of course, if you have multiple children this can become a real challenge. However, the payoff is enormous and the cost of failure high. Enjoy making the time and focus on the joy. Again, this may seem obvious. That is because you already do this when you are communicating successfully. I am simply asking if you can do it better and more often.

The Listening Advantage Exercise

On a separate sheet of paper write down several times as a child when you were proud of your behavior or of solving a problem. Now write down several times when you were proud of your own child's decision making. Did you as a parent allow that to happen? Were silence and listening involved? A parent who wants to be a great listener and a great communicator is always searching for opportunities to listen. These can be spontaneous but they can also be ritualized. Putting aside time at the start of each morning, or at some time each day, to listen attentively can be powerful. It develops the habit of listening in the parent and by example, in the child. A child can who develops the practice of listening becomes a great communicator. However, great communication skills are not the only positive result of listening skills. Great thinking skills and creativity can also be inspired by parents. The parent can, for example, act as a catalyst by asking good questions such as "What was the most interesting thing that happened today?" "Did anything make you happy today?" "Did anything make you sad today?" "Did you ask any good questions today?" Likewise family meetings, car trips, and the bedtime ritual can all offer opportunities for ritualized communication.

Finally, when you have multiple children, time set aside for each child individually rather than with the others can be important. In our own family we have periodic Josh days, Jamie days, and Alex days. They are not as often as we would like but the kids crave them. On this day we set aside time to spend specifically with that child. As children grow older it is especially important to involve the child in constructing the day—where will you go, what will you do? Get your child to co-produce the memories they will have of spending time with you as a child.

"Listening Is Different for Everyone" Exercise

When we are actually listening and aware, we have a tendency to think of it as an absolute experience. We believe that what we hear is what everyone hears. You may be surprised. Ask everyone in the family to be silent and to listen and to notice as many sounds as possible. After a few minutes stop and compare lists. Did everyone hear the same things? Were there things one of you heard that another did not? We all think we hear the same things, but it is a question of focus.

Conclusion

Maintaining silence and listening are skills to be developed. They enhance your powers as a parent and communicator and help to grow great self-reliant kids. Like all skills, however, they must be practiced. When we are quiet and listen we learn a great deal. Our children often use the silence we provide to "think out loud" in a way that we might never have a chance to observe if we simply fill the silence with our suggestions.

Being silent and developing our listening skills also allows our children to develop independence and problem solving skills, and to feel respected.

Reminders and Actions

- Ask children of all ages questions that encourage them to review their problems and to suggest their own answers. When possible, ask questions that make the process of problem solving fun and enjoyable. Examples: "How would you solve that problem if you were a millionaire? If you were poor?" "Have you ever seen anyone do a good job in that situation?"
- Ask questions and give the child the opportunity to devel-

op judgment and skills in selecting between possible solutions. Examples: "How do *you* make your best choices?"
- Practice listening carefully and noticing how the child conveys information and how the child makes decisions. This can help you to guide the child more effectively in making morally correct and socially responsible decisions.
- Listening gives you insight into how your child processes information. This will give you a chance to learn to know your child and to customize communication.
- Provide ritual opportunities for listening.

Chapter

7

Make Your Communication Outcome-Based

"Men stumble over truth from time to time,
but most pick themselves up and continue
on as if nothing happened."

—Prime Minister Sir Winston Churchill

A s a general rule, success in any endeavor requires that we have clarity of purpose—that we know the outcome we desire. Indeed, in earlier chapters we examined the value of having a clear plan of communication. In fact, in the workplace the concept of outcome-based communication is widely accepted and practiced. Before a meeting the meeting's moderator or leader almost always tries to clarify what it is that he or she would like to accomplish. This can be achieved by developing and refining an agenda or through a combination of other techniques.

When a corporate officer or manager communicates with employees, the manager's communication is always most effective when she has thought out in advance what she would like to accomplish through that conversation or memorandum. The concept of outcome-based communication, or knowing what you want in advance, is rarely, however, applied consciously in the family setting.

Clearly, time spent alone with children spontaneously playing, reading, or interacting without a scripted result in mind is one of the great pleasures and essences of life. Indulge in it regularly. Be present in the moment and forget about outcomes, results, and goals. However, when you have an important task to accomplish with a child, a teen, or an adult child, outcome- based communication makes all the sense in the world. If you are approaching a young child to help them develop good study habits, to clean their room, or to alter or avoid a negative behavior, outcome-based communication can often be the key. When you are helping teenage children to develop the confidence and good decision-making skills to avoid violence, drugs, and alcohol, then successful outcome-based communication is a responsibility. Effective persuasion is essential.

And when you are approaching an adult child to discuss some family interaction or family matter, it is important that your goals be clear to you before commencing the communication.

Outcome-based communication is not only appropriate in such situations but also is highly effective. If you approach a young child simply with the general idea that you would like them to clean their room more often or do their homework rather than watching television, the conversation could quickly deteriorate into an argument, scolding, or an ineffective reprimand.

If you ask a teenager to help with something around the house, but it's not really clear when this must be accomplished, it is easy for the teen to put it off. They don't think they are doing anything wrong. It is not a priority to them, so they forget. And you get angry. This may become a pattern which is unlikely to get you the desired result, a result which no doubt you think would be beneficial to the child as well. As soon as the parent starts "the speech," the child shuts down or argues back. Both sides solidify their positions. The end result is that neither parent nor child is happy.

There is a better alternative. If you carefully think out the goal you desire and are specific as to when it must be done, your odds of success rise rapidly. If you consider how you can appeal to the child's own interest and motivate them, and if you have a backup plan for communication, then you are much more likely to get the result you seek. In addition, if you imagine yourself engaged successfully in this communication, before it ever starts, or imagine yourself failing and consider how you will maintain calm if that happens, then you are much more likely to be successful even if you meet resistance. In NLP they call this "future pacing." In theater they call it rehearsal. In this case, you improve the result when you use your imagination to rehearse. You may discover flaws in your own approach. You can anticipate objections and deal with them. You are prepared for an initial failure. All of this will make you more flexible and much more likely to achieve your result.

Additionally, if you realize that not all kids process language in the same way, you can tailor your words and your approach to that child. If you carefully observe their reaction you are even more likely to get an outcome that benefits you and your child. See "Tailor Your Communication" in Chapter 10.

Because you have planned you will have clarity of purpose. Because you have planned you will customize the message to that child. Because you have cultivated flexibility you will be creative if objections are raised. In short, you radically improve your odds of success. Rapport, flexibility, and attention or acuity are essential to outcome-based communication. So be sure to read Chapters 8, 9, and 10.

Conclusion
Outcome-based communication can be a highly effective tool in family communication.

Knowing what you desire, before you commence a communication, and having a backup plan if the communication does not go as desired, can provide dramatically better results than unplanned communication.

Reminders and Actions
- Once you have decided on the goal of a communication, consider your approach and how the child may react. Be prepared to be flexible and to adapt.
- Have a backup plan, or two, or three.

- Practice remaining calm and working methodically toward your desired result.
- Remember that spontaneous, unplanned time with children is desirable and wonderful but careful and planned communication at other times can make your lives together time even more enjoyable.
- Register at www.successtechnologies.com or www.redwirepress.com and request our Brain Booster Bibliography, articles, or updates on parenting topics as they are published. If you are not a computer person send a self-addressed, stamped envelope to STI, P. O. Box 507, Malvern, Pennsylvania 19355 to request them.

8

Building Rapport

"Ahhhhhhhh that feels great. Don't repeat that to yourself day and night . . . because you might."

—David Frees, Acapulco International Conference, 2001

Communication is always more effective when the person you are communicating with likes you, enjoys your company, is amused by you, or simply gets that warm, fuzzy feeling. There are techniques you can use to build rapport that make you more likeable to people and which therefore make it more likely that your communications will be well received. Think about this in your own experience. Haven't there been times when you met somebody and instantly felt close to them? When they spoke to you (or more likely listened to you), they seemed a little more interesting than other people, a little more fascinating, a little more intelligent, and you paid a little closer attention to what it was they were saying.

Sometimes when we meet someone like this they will confess to us that they are having the same experience. Many times they are not consciously aware of it. They just feel good. That is a nice environment in which to communicate, to teach, to make suggestions, or even to "give orders." Now that you remember times like this, ask yourself, "Would this be a nice feeling to have while communicating with my child or children?" "Would they be more receptive and more likely to share information with me?"

Now it may seem strange to think about building rapport in a family situation. We tend to assume that rapport just exists. Most of the literature of rapport examines the techniques of rapport in the business setting or as they apply to sales. After all, our family members already like us—don't they? Well first of all I'm sure you will acknowledge that there are times when you feel more or less rapport with your spouse, friends, and children. And, it is through contrast that we really appreciate experiences. I am not proposing a blissful never-never land where there is no strain in these relationships. Rather, I am suggesting that if you look back at the times when you were in beautiful rapport with a child, there are things that were consistently present. I can imagine that you might like to have this rapport more often. I can also believe your children might like to learn that skill from you. But to have rapport more often, you need to be aware of the factors or circumstances that lead to rapport.

So how do the experts believe that we create, enhance, and maintain rapport? The essence of building rapport quickly and easily can be summarized in a couple of skills.

The first is to develop mental and sensory acuity. For example, remember to listen to how other people speak, and watch how they breathe. Watch their overall body posture and match that with your own. Literally match your breathing to theirs. As they breathe in, so do you. As they breathe out—you do, too. The unconscious mind notices this. It tells them that you are like them. They relax into rapport with you.

In my seminars, I often tell this story to illustrate rapport skills. In my practice, I call lawyers in other states to help me with projects. I am from Pennsylvania. Those other lawyers are often from the South. When I am speaking to one of my corresponding counsels from North Carolina, I do not quickly rattle off all of my needs and desires and demand they be met instantaneously. Rather, I speak more slowly and in the manner of my co-counsel. I am patient. I pause. It is harder on the phone, of course. When you are face to face with someone you can stand the way they are standing, breathe the way they are breathing, use eye contact the way they are using eye contact. On the phone I can still use the same tone of voice and the same speed of speech as the other person. I can make my voice similar to their own. I may even begin to adopt their accent. Has that ever happened to you? This may seem silly, but the fact of the matter is that it works. The other person's unconscious mind is monitoring all of these factors and when your behavior matches the pattern that the other person likes, enjoys, and uses themselves they feel more at ease. Their unconscious mind is going to say "I like this person" and your communication is more likely to be well received. When you give people reasons to trust you, they are less critical, and more likely to listen attentively. Most of us think logically about trust. However, we usually make an emotional decision that we like someone and trust them, then we rationalize this decision with logical thoughts about why we trust them.

However, you don't have to take my word for it or search for scientific evidence to support this. The next time you're speaking to a spouse, partner, or child—try it. Match your breathing, gestures, body posture, expressions, and tone of voice to theirs. If they are enthusiastic, match their enthusiasm.

Pay close attention whenever you feel in rapport naturally. What is going on? Notice what happens when you match breathing, body posture, and voice. Isn't that better?

Occasionally people have said to me "That is manipulative!" The last time someone said that to me in front of a large group, I asked her to come forward and stand next to me. I noticed that her name tag said "Nancy." Yet throughout the conversation, I kept referring to her as "Janet." Each time I did it she became increasingly frustrated until finally she blurted out, "My name is Nancy!" I said "Oh, I actually realized that Janet, but I was wondering if I should communicate with you in a way that seemed easy and natural so that you could pay attention to what I said or in a way that was distracting and irritating so that you didn't even hear what I said. I was wondering, Nancy, which would be more effective?" Of course, she laughed a little and conceded that she hadn't been paying much attention to what I said. My mistake about her name was a distraction. This is the essence and secret of rapport skills. You can communicate with people in a way that is unnatural or difficult for them or in a way that is relaxing for them and makes the communication easier for them to understand. It is your choice. But first you have to use your observational skills to discover what they like.

Remember also that *all communication is manipulation.* There is never a time when you speak to someone, write to someone, or give someone a hand signal (rude or otherwise) when you are not attempting to manipulate them in some way. When you ask someone for something, you are hoping that they will provide it to you. When you give them information you are hoping they will use it in a certain way. When you ask a child to clean his or her room you are hoping they will do that. You may want them to build good habits. Your motivation is good but you are manipulating when you speak. The important thing is the integrity with which you use your communication skills. If all communication is manipulation then be clear on the purpose of your communication and be clear that your purpose is valid and ethical.

Conclusion

Whenever we communicate we have a choice to make. We can communicate in the way that we enjoy or in the way that the recipient will most enjoy. When we communicate in a way designed to engage, entertain, and enthrall the recipients of our communication we are much more likely to get the results we desire. In other words, we can do it the easy way or the hard way. By becoming aware of how your children communicate, and the type of communication they enjoy as well as how they process language, you can build a greater rapport with them not only for what you are trying to communicate to them right now, but for your whole lives together. Communication is always more effective when the person with whom you are speaking enjoys your communication and trusts you.

Reminders and Actions

- Remember to develop mental and sensory acuity and agility. Be flexible and become more aware of how your children speak and what type of language they seem to enjoy.
- Listen to others and watch how they breathe. Breathe with them.
- Children (and people generally) tend to favor one way of processing information. We all use our auditory, visual, and kinesthetic senses to perceive the world. Become aware of which of the modes your child is using and favors right now, and deliver your message in a way that is consistent with it.
- Register at www.successtechnologies.com and request our NLP/Hypnosis Bibliography, for more information on the work of Dr. Richard Bandler, John Grinder, Robert Dilts, John LaValle, and other NLP greats.

Part Three

The Tactics, Tools, and Skills of
Effective Parent/Child Communication

"Happiness is the natural flower of duty."
—Phillip Brooks

Introduction to
Part Three

Remember that there are ways to think strategically about the language of parenting and then there are the actual tactics to be used. The strategies are the big-picture things, the mindset and beliefs. We discussed them earlier.

For example, remember that all communication should be *outcome-based*. You should have a clear understanding of what it is you want when you speak to a child or an adult. Are you asking for something or trying to teach—The purpose of your communication, what you desire, should be clear to you first. Also, on a strategic level, you need to **be congruent**. Much of communication is based not on the words we select but on the way we speak, the way we use our bodies, the way we use our language, the way we breathe, and the tone, and pace of our speech. When all of these factors agree our meaning is clear to our children, our spouses, and others. When these factors conflict, most children (and adults) notice the message conveyed in tone and gestures not just the words. They do that because language is full of noise. Many of us attribute different meanings to the same words. For this reason, we need to ask questions after speaking to be sure that we are being understood.

Another strategic concept is the need to see communication as a process. Because our relationships are always changing we must cultivate flexibility and develop our **sensory acuity**. We need to be aware of what is going on when we speak. Are people understanding us? If it appears not (and we may be wrong about that), we simply need to check with them.[17] If they do not yet understand what we intended then we need to be flexible and try something else. Once we have developed our acuity we can see how we need to adapt and then change our behavior.

If we notice that something is not working we need to be able and willing to change techniques and try something different. This is where the techniques of this chapter can really come in handy; if one is not working another may be available and usable. Finally, remember to cultivate positive and useful beliefs about yourself as a communicator. Remember the times in your life when you were a great communicator—think about that and be aware that there are times when you have communicated elegantly, beautifully, and succinctly. When you cultivate these beliefs your results will begin to radically improve.

In this section we examine the tactics of effective parent/child communication. These are specific techniques, tools, and linguistic devices you can use to enhance any communication. However, they should be employed in the course of using the larger strategies. Any tactic employed without consideration of the fundamentals of communication is likely to fail. However, once you realize that you are already a great communicator and when you commit to using the principles outlined in Part One and Part Two of the book —then the tactics of communication can really begin to improve your results. The more tactics you have the more flexible and confident you become. If one doesn't work you move on to the next always being guided by the larger strategies. Here is a brief list of tactics which can be employed to the mutual delight of parents and children of all ages:

Avoiding negation

Tailoring your communication to the individual

Remembering to agree

Getting them thinking about resources

Creating a model of creativity

Using embedded suggestions

Having a sense of humor

Using presuppositions

Using tag questions

Chapter

9

Avoiding Negation

"To repeat what others have said requires intelligence; to challenge it requires brains."

—Mary Pettibond Poole

It is common, from the time our children are very young to employ negation as a way of attempting to teach them or to give them "orders." We say, "Don't spill the milk." We say, "Don't forget your lunch," or "Don't forget your homework." And later we say "Don't forget your wallet." "Don't forget the car keys." "Don't forget to call." In each of these cases we may inadvertently be defeating our own goal of clear and effective communication. How?

Well, when I say to you "Don't think of the color blue!" what happens? What do you immediately think of? Doesn't a big blue dot or big blue square or some other big blue thing flash into your mind? It does. That is because of the way our minds work to process language. We all need to make a picture or somehow represent the thing we are thinking of before we can negate it. The spoken word is a pattern of vibrations, which moves into our ear canal, and then down to the eardrum where the vibrations cause the drum to move. The drum in turn moves the bones in the inner ear. These movements are converted into electro-chemical reactions within the brain. Our mind does not actually hear the sound. It "hears" a representation of the sound. While science can explain things to this point it is not so clear to science "who" or "what" actually watches the internal representation of the words or vibration. But we do make an internal representation of what we hear.

So when we say to our young children "Don't spill the milk," or "Don't eat any cookies while I am gone," they *must* imagine themselves engaging in the undesirable behavior before they can negate it. When you say, "Don't spill the milk!" there are times when you can actually see their hands beginning to shake. Notice that I said "avoid negation." I didn't say "Don't negate!" When I say "avoid negation" notice how that feels and what your mind does. You see yourself avoiding something that is bad or is negative. You are making your way around it. You are avoiding it—and that is the desired outcome. Now notice what happens if I say "Don't think of the color blue." It is a very different feeling. Which feeling would you like to give your children? Knowing this, which would you say: "Don't do drugs!" or "To stay healthy enjoy avoiding drugs," or "Can you imagine feeling good by staying away from drugs?" Remember when you speak this way, the mind cannot process your words without imagining feeling good *without* drugs.

This new ability is something that takes some *practice* so remember to catch yourself when you do use negation and remember to practice ways of avoiding it. I know this works. One time I was standing in my driveway and I saw my young son, Alex, running toward the street. My first thought was to say, "Don't run into the street." However, you know how time often seems to slow down in circumstances like these, and I actually seemed to have time in my mind to say it another way. So instead I said "Stop right there **on the grass**!" Alex did just that. He slammed on the brakes and actually looked down to see if he was still standing on the grass. Had I said "Don't run into street!" he may have stopped but his mind would have certainly been making a picture of himself running into the street before he could negate that.

This little tactic is more powerful than you may imagine. My oldest son, Josh, who occasionally would come to my seminars or listen to me speak to people about these matters, came home from school once when he was in the fourth grade and said "Dad, I am really mad at Ms. Williams." I knew that this was odd because he loved school and he loved Ms. Williams.

"What's bothering you, Josh?" I said, and he said, "Well, Ms. Williams keeps saying to the class 'Don't forget your homework.' " "Well, Josh what's the matter with that?" I asked. "You see, Dad, when she says 'Don't forget your homework' everybody makes a picture of themselves forgetting their homework and then they leave it at home. I mean they are mentally practicing what she doesn't want them to do."

"Well what are you going to do about that, Josh?" "Don't worry," he said, "I've already taken care of it." Now that is either alarming or very exciting for a parent to hear. I wasn't at all sure what Josh had done. "What exactly did you say to Ms. Williams?" I tried to ask nonchalantly (yet congruently nonchalantly). "Oh, I went up to her after class and I said, 'Ms. Williams, what happens when I say to you "Don't think of the color yellow?' " "That's odd, Josh, I do— I think of the color yellow." "Oh," I said to Josh, "what did you say then?" I said, "That's R-I-G-H-T." "Did you say anything else, Josh?" "No, I trust that her unconscious mind will figure it out."

That may seem like a funny little story but the truth of the matter is, that if Josh is to be believed, Ms. Williams did begin to say "Remember your homework" after that and more kids *did* remember to bring it in. You don't have to take my word or Josh's word for this. Experiment with it. Have fun and see for yourself.

Where else might this be useful? Have you ever said to your husband or wife, "Don't forget this" or "Don't forget that"? From now on remember to catch yourself when you do it. Remember to improve your language and see if it works. Now I don't know if you will begin doing this as soon as you put this book down or whether you will begin doing it effectively, smoothly, and easily over the next few days or weeks. However, I do imagine that you will start doing this. Catch yourself and become pleasantly surprised by what you discover. Remember: If you have a successful, humorous, or delightful experience with this or any of the other tactics in this book, you are welcome to call me at 1-800-769-5454 or e-mail me at dfrees@successtechnologies.com and tell us your story. If I use your story to illustrate some points in a future edition of this book or in any of my books I will be happy to send you a free book and I will include you in the acknowledgments when the book is published.

Conclusion

Because of the way the human mind processes language, when we negate or tell a child "Don't spill the milk" or "Don't forget your homework," we are causing them to mentally rehearse the very behavior we wish them to avoid. For example, if I say "Don't think of the color blue," what immediately pops into your mind? For this reason, we should seek to avoid negation and state our requests in the positive or in a manner that requires the child, in processing our language, to rehearse the desired behavior.

Reminders and Actions

- Remember to avoid negation.
- Remember to practice stating requests in the positive. For example, "Don't spill the milk" becomes "Keep the milk in the cup," and "Don't forget your homework" becomes "Remember to bring your homework home and to do it." An even better option might be "Remember to enjoy bringing your homework home and getting it done as soon as possible."[18]
- Remember to catch yourself when you negate so that you can begin to comfortably change your pattern.

- Remember to catch yourself when you successfully use the new way of speaking.
- Register at www.successtechnologies.com or send a self-addressed, stamped envelope to Success Technologies, Inc., P. O. Box 507, Malvern, Pennsylvania 19355 to request a free wallet card or download the wallet card.pdf. Remember to browse our articles and submit your own communication skill stories for upcoming books.

Chapter

10

Tailor Your
Communication

*"All generalizations are both useful and
dangerous—including this one."*

—Author Robert Anton Wilson

Many self-help books, business seminars, and assessment tools help us to improve our management and understanding of others by dividing people into several broad categories. For example, the Meyers-Briggs Type Indicator (MBTI®) classifies people as Extroverted/Introverted, Sensing/Intuition, Thinking/ Feeling, and Judgmental/Perceiving. Other systems sort people into thinkers, workers, and enactors. Still others group people into visual, kinesthetic, or auditory categories. While this type of pigeonholing does serve the valuable purpose of helping us to target ourselves more effectively in a complex world, such categories really constitute overgeneralizations.

As Robert Anton Wilson once observed "All generalizations are both useful and dangerous—including this one."

If we want to be truly effective communicators especially with our children and other family members, we need to be aware of how we process information and how our family members are processing our language and information. We also need, whenever possible, to customize our communications in order to make that processing comfortable, easy to remember, and of a nature that makes people involved want to act upon our suggestions. At first customizing communication may seem hard. However, it can quickly become enjoyable, effective and even fun.

To assist you in this process we will begin with some generalizations and then see how we can use them to carefully customize our speech. All of us process the information about the outside world which comes into our mind and body through our five primary senses—sight, hearing, touch, taste, and our sense of smell. Children and adults alike tend to process verbal communication primarily through three of the senses: the visual, auditory, and kinesthetic senses. In fact, at any given moment they will tend to concentrate on just one of these three. In other words, they tend to focus on pictures triggered by the sounds of speech, on the sounds themselves, or on feelings generated by the sounds. When I say this, however, I am not saying that people tend to be "visual people," "feeling people," or "hearing people." Rather, I am saying that children and adults tend to favor one way of analyzing speech at any given time. We all switch among the three ways of processing information.

Sometimes people tend to focus on one and while that is useful to note it is also important to realize that a child will not always use the visual way of analyzing your language, the kinesthetic way of analyzing your language, or the auditory system. They switch.

Again the system of neurolinguistic programming developed by Richard Bandler and John Grinder drew upon the fields of linguistics and psychology to study the way in which people process conversations and verbal communications. Bandler and Grinder found that people gave signals in their speech as well as nonverbal cues about how they were processing the language they were receiving.[19]

For example, if a child is focused on listening to you and processing the sound of your voice they will often say "Oh, I hear what you are saying." An adult might say "That *rings* true to me," "That *rings* a bell," or "That *clicks* for me." These are clues in the child's or adult's speech that they are actually listening to what you are saying and processing it through the auditory system.

Another child or adult might say "That seems fuzzy to me." They might also say "That's clear as mud," or "I see what you mean." These are all indicators that the child is listening to your words but converting them into visual images and analyzing their content primarily by using the visual sense. While it seems strange when you think about it, how often have you heard someone say "Oh, I see what you are saying." They are describing the process they are going through—they are hearing your words and converting them into some visual format.

Children or adults who are processing verbal information in a kinestetic way or in predominately kinesthetic way, might say to you, "That doesn't feel right to me." They might also say, "I have a bad gut reaction to that," or "That gives me a funny feeling." In this case, they are again taking in your words through their sense of hearing but they are judging your words or experiencing them through the feelings or sensations created in their body.

Now again, remember that while a child or adult may primarily process verbal information through one of those three senses, the chances are that they are simultaneously experiencing the information with all three senses. They are tending to emphasize one at a particular moment. For that reason, you may notice that a child signals visual processing at one time and kinesthetic or auditory at another. You may notice yourself that when you are at a concert you are so focused on the sound of the instruments or the voices that you pay no attention to your kinesthetic sensations. You may forget how comfortable or uncomfortable the seat you are sitting in is. You may also notice that when you are in an art gallery looking at paintings, the sound of other people around you seems to fade away. The sound of course is still there but you are focusing on the visual input you are receiving.

Now like so many other things, with verbal communication, we can either try to do it the easy way or the hard way. When you are aware that a child is processing information in a visual way, it may be desirable to begin communicating with them by using visual communication. If you describe a situation to a child and they say "I can't see what you mean," you probably don't want to just describe it to them again or, demand that they listen. Rather, you might consider drawing them a picture or a diagram as a tool to explaining it. You might also say to them, "Does that seem clearer to you now?" or "Can you see more clearly what I mean?" In this way you are indicating to their unconscious mind that you are aware of how they are processing information and you are attempting to communicate in the easiest and most efficient way for them.

Likewise, if a child says to you that they are hearing what the teacher is saying but they get a funny feeling about it, you might want to explore with them situations where they have heard what the teacher says and have a good feeling. You might also begin to realize that this child might be processing information in a primarily kinesthetic way. This is useful for children for example who are learning to spell. Some children who process words visually have difficulty with phonetic spelling. Other children who process information in a primarily kinesthetic way may have trouble spelling because they do not feel the letters. In this case, we might suggest filling a plastic bag with some ketchup and having them write on the bag with their fingers so that they can actually feel the letters and see them. In fact, if you have the child feel the letters, see the letters, and say the letters to themselves at the same time, you may find that their retention soars. This brings us to another point.[20]

Just because a child finds it simplest, easiest, and maybe most enjoyable to process verbal information through one of these three senses, many scientific studies and our own experience tell us that a child will retain and recall information better when they experience and learn that information using multiple modalities. Think about it—that is why teachers will often write on the board so that the children can see it. They will then have the children repeat what they have written so they are saying it, and then have the children write the information down so that they are feeling it or connecting the information with the kinesthetic sense.

Therefore, when we want a child to have good recall of the information that we are teaching, we may want to initially customize our communication with the child to build rapport and make them aware that we are sensitive to how they process information. For a higher level of recall, we may want to have the child experience the information in multiple ways, and to make the information sound or seem outrageous! The more unusual, the more easily recalled.

For example, my children always use their spelling words in outrageous multi-sensory sentences. I encourage them to make up sentences using the words and involving sounds, smells and visuals. You get the picture. This can be done at any age and with any type of information.

It doesn't just apply to spelling words or later the periodic table. If you make your communication multi-sensory and even outrageous (when recall is really important) you will find that your children can and happily will remember.

There are many other ways in which children and adults process information. Some children enjoy bright atmospheres, others can listen to music while they study though to a sibling that would be a distraction. Your job is to *become aware* and to use that new knowledge to become a better communicator. Dr. Robert Arnot, M.D., reminds us in his book *The Biology of Success*, "If you want to be happy and motivated, if you want to maximize your potential and be consistently 'in the zone,' you have to know your brain type and understand other brain types."

Conclusion

Be aware of the verbal and nonverbal ways in which your children tell you how they process information. Use that knowledge to customize your communication with each child so that it is done in a way that makes them feel rapport with you and feel comfortable. We generally process information through three senses: our visual, auditory, and kinesthetic senses. When we communicate with them people tend to give us clues about how they like to learn and process information. If we notice the clues and build rapport, our children will feel better and listen more attentively. Then we can introduce a child to learning in multiple ways, the information is likely to be retained longer and be easier to recall, and the child will build a good lifelong learning habit.

Reminders and Actions

- Practice catching your own verbal indicators of how you process information.
- Look for the indicators of how your kids learn.
- Engage in conversations where you have family members learn information using all three modalities. For example, rather than say "Do you see that now?" say "How

does that look to you?" and follow it up with "Does that answer feel correct?" and "Can you repeat back to me how that sounded to you?"

- Devise learning tools for your children to experience learning in kinesthetic, visual, and auditory ways.
- Visit www.successtechnologies.com, check out our articles, and register for information and newsletters. You can also email a request for the NLP Bibliography, for much more information on the modalities and strategies of communication and rapport skills.
- NOTE: For more information on the unconscious aspects of communication read *My Voice Will Go with You* by Milton Erickson and for more about the strategies of learning read *Dynamic Learning* by Dilts and Epstein.

Chapter

11

Using
Presuppositions

"The mind stretched to a new idea never
goes back to its original dimension."

—Supreme Court Justice Oliver Wendell Holmes

I t is common for parents to report to me that they are frustrated by a child who is uncertain of his or her own skills and powers. As you may recall, at first when I was faced with a refusal by an adult or a child I would argue with them. I would in essence argue for their own empower-ment. If a child said, "I can't." I would say "Yes you can!" However, I was arguing with them and that placed a barrier between us. Presuppositions help us to solve this problem. For example, when you say to a child, "Would you please clean your room?" "Would you please do your homework?" or "Would you please finish that project?" their response may be to say, "I can't do that." How can presuppositions be used to solve this problem?

The first reaction of most parents is often to argue with the child, to cite the many reasons why the parent believes that the child *can* do it. That, however, is just the point. It is the parent's belief and not the child's. A better approach is to utilize presupposition in your language. You can *agree* with the child by saying "I know that you feel you can't just yet." This may have a fascinating result. You have agreed with the child that they can't do it (or at least that they feel that way). However, the simple insertion of the words "just yet" suggests to the child that they will be able to in the future. This is far more discreet than a direct confrontation with the child or a direct refutation of the child's position. It allows the child to consider the possibility of success and to develop a new belief in their own skills. They have already done it in their minds. You were merely the catalyst.

Sometimes when a child refuses to do something it is because he or she lacks confidence or belief in themselves. The question that asks "What would have to happen in order for you to be able to do _____?", or for a younger child "What would happen if you did do it?" is also supportive of the child. It acknowledges their feeling that they cannot currently do it. But it also asks them a resourceful question. It asks them to review their resources and determine what would have to be different in order for them to be able to. Be aware, as a parent, that the child may choose either not to answer or to say "Nothing would have to happen. I just can't do it." Be encouraged to know, however, that the child cannot even understand your question without making an internal image or representation of themselves doing it. This is likely to be helpful and to advance their belief in themselves and their self-confidence. It is again, a form of presupposition. The question itself presupposes there are things that if they happened would make it possible for the child to do it.

Again we recall the example of a color. Even if I say to you, "Don't think of the color blue," the color blue immediately leaps into your mind. You have to envision it in order to understand my sentence. The same is true with your discreet presupposition regarding the child's abilities. You have not argued with the child or told them they could do the thing that they refused. Rather, you have asked them to tell you what would have to happen, what resources they would have to have, in order to be able to do it. They must imagine themselves doing it in order to understand your question.

Of course, we would be happiest if the child simply rattled off a list of things that would enable them to perform that task. While that is not always the case, it is likely that our question will cause less confrontation between parent and child and it will get the child thinking the right way.

Let's consider a few additional examples of presupposition. If a child is having a music lesson, for example, and throws down the music in disgust and says, "I can't do this," "I'll never learn this," or "This makes me so mad," the initial reaction is to confront the child. Well-intentioned parents usually say, "We are paying good money for you to take these lessons" or "You aren't trying hard enough." Or they will exaggerate the child's ability by saying "You are doing so well," when in fact, the child may not be doing well at all.

Presupposition and agreement, however, are tools that encourage and support the child in a way that draws on the child's own resources.

The parent, rather than arguing, may simply observe, "I can tell that you are frustrated now, but can you imagine how you will feel when you *do* learn this?" Again the question presupposes the child's ability. It also recognizes that the child may need to do things differently in the future. By asking the child to use their imagination we are simply asking them to engage in something that is less difficult or confrontational than trying to play the piece perfectly at this time.

If their refusal or frustration is with cleaning their room, you can again ask "Can you imagine what you could do to this room to make yourself feel better?" To return to the music example for a moment, one could also say "I don't know whether it would take you more practice today or more practice over the next few weeks to do this well, but how will you feel when you *have* improved?" Again this presupposes improvement and does not try to define the precise road to improvement for the child. It also presupposes improvement might be fast or come more slowly. It allows a choice. Remember, after each of these it is desirable to be quiet and allow the child to speak.

Often the child will leave a silent space in the conversation, expecting you to leap back in and confront them. *Do not fall for this bait.* Rather, allow the silence to continue. The child, understanding that you are reflecting respect for them and giving them time to think may fill in the silence on their own and begin to raise issues about the music lessons, cleaning their room, or whatever else that may have never been raised. Furthermore, the child may come to good decisions and conclusions on their own. Again, this has all occurred in an environment that you have helped to create and facilitate.

So far, we have been considering how you can use presuppositions in a positive way to help a child to discover strengths and adopt a better attitude. However, you should also become alert to how your child uses presuppositions in their own speech. Presuppositions reflect underlying assumptions by the child of which she may not even be consciously aware. For example, a child may say, "That teacher is as bad as Mrs. Higgins."

In this case, the child's presupposition is that Mrs. Higgins is bad. However, it might be important for you, as a parent, to know more. Exactly how is Mrs. Higgins bad? Does the child consider Mrs. Higgins to be bad as a teacher or as a person? Having identified in what capacity, you might then want to know what made the child think of her as "bad." If she says "I can't understand her. I can't seem to hear her," we are already learning a lot more. We may, in this way, learn things about our children and help them to discover things that make us more effective parents and our children happier people and more effective students.

Another example would be a child who says "I'm worse than Tom." The presupposition is that Tom is bad at something. What is it? Why does the child think Tom is bad? How does the child consider himself to be worse? Only by getting at the presupposition is the parent able to become consciously aware of the perceived limitation and only then can the parent help the child.

Be aware of your presuppositions and your children's use of presuppositions.

Conclusion

The use of presuppositions is a very effective and natural way to empower children. When a child says he can't do something or refuses to do it, our natural tendency as parents is to argue with him. With presupposition we can be in apparent agreement with our child, yet gently suggest that they are more powerful than they had imagined. For example, if a child says "I can't clean up my room" we can say "Yes you can and do it now"—which puts us in direct opposition to the child. Or we can say, "I know that you feel that you can't just yet. However, what would have to happen in order for you to do it without complaining and maybe even while having fun?"

> *"Faith is to believe what you do not yet see; the reward for faith is to see what you believe."* (emphasis added)

—Saint Augustine

Reminders and Actions

- I don't know whether you will begin using presuppositions today or whether you will just think about it for a few days. Notice that this presupposes that you will do it.
- Presuppositions acknowledge the child's feeling that they can't do something but gently suggest that they will be able to.
- When using presuppositions, you acknowledge that the child may wish to begin now to do something or may not wish to do so for a few more days. You give the child a certain element of choice, but your presupposition has suggested that they will be able to do it shortly.
- For the child who likes to refuse, or do the opposite of what you are suggesting, remember that you can use the negative. If I say "Don't think of the color blue," blue leaps to your mind. Likewise if you say "Don't clean your room just yet," you are creating a presupposition that they will and actually having them rehearse doing it.

12

Remember to Agree

"Children need models rather than critics."

—Joseph Joubert, *Pensees*, 1842

It used to be that when someone disagreed with me I would go right on disagreeing with them. If I asked one of my children to do something, for instance, and they told me "No, I can't do that," I would simply say, "Yes, you can!" I would be enthusiastic. I would be supportive. I would give them all of the reasons why I thought they could do it.

I thought that this was good parenting and good communication. I thought that I was being a good teacher and that my reasoning would be clear and persuasive. After all, I believed in my children's abilities. However, put yourself in the child's position. When someone disagrees with you, you put up barriers and start thinking of all of the reasons why you are right and they are wrong. When you tell a child that they can do something, your expectations may be at variance with their sense of their own skills. This puts you at odds with your child, no matter how supportive you intended to be. There is, however, a solution to this problem. The solution is a powerful one. It is an interesting one. Kids love it, adults love it, and it is respectful and encouraging in a natural way. It has a strange name. It is called AGREEMENT!

Now, when I ask someone to do something and they tell me that they can't, I simply agree. I say, "I know you can't yet." Or, "I know that you can't right now." Notice those words "yet" and "right now." They are presuppositions. When we say, "I know you can't yet," it presupposes that at some point in the future they will be able to. It is hard for a child or an adult for that matter to disagree with this. The fact is that you are agreeing with them. You are acknowledging that they don't believe that they can do it—just yet.

As I have mentioned throughout this book, the use of presuppositions, creates in the mind the possibility that they will be able to at some point. In fact, it is a gentle way of saying that you believe in them and you believe that they will be able to. It suggests that the two of you have the same beliefs. Sometimes that is enough and the child will say "Oh" and go on to be more cooperative. However, whether it is a child or an adult family member there may be more resistance. I often ask the question "What would have to happen in order for you be able to do it now?" With young kids I will often say, "I know you can't yet, but if you could do it how would you do it?" This is an interesting sentence. It asks them to use their imagination. Imagination usually involves something happening in the future. It is more distant, not quite so threatening, and not quite so daunting.

Furthermore, it is not asking them to actually do it, it is just asking them to imagine it. So when children say "I can't," and I say "I know you can't yet, but what if you could do it?" it is not uncommon for them to roll their eyes around and scrunch their faces up and make fun of imagining. Then magically, they give me an answer. They actually tell me what would have to happen, what they would need, and how they would feel. This is a major breakthrough. They have gone from "no" to describing how they will do it. Fascinating. Try it.

The use of presuppositions and imagination are not the only ways in which we can improve communication through agreement. If we create an environment where we encourage our children when young and perhaps even more extensively as older children to contribute their ideas to the family, it is inevitable that they will come up with ideas that are for one reason or another impractical or with which we simply disagree. However, an outright disagreement with a child of any age who is attempting to contribute could have the effect of discouraging their participation and contribution to the family. For that reason, it is important again to begin by agreeing. It is almost always possible to find one or two reasons why an idea may have merit. If you thank a child for their contribution and explain the reasons why it may have merit and then a reason why you disagree with it, you have acknowledged their contribution. It is also useful when disagreeing to request their input on some other factor. So for example, if a child suggested that you go on a family vacation to a place that was just too expensive or impractical, you might say "That would be wonderful and I know that we would all enjoy it." You might add, "That would be a special trip and we would have to have more time to plan and save for that. But tell me, what is it that you would most enjoy about that trip? And "How could we get those things in a trip closer to home?" In *Make Peace with Anyone*, David Lieberman, Ph.D, suggests that even when you disagree with someone you should always 1) show appreciation for the input; 2) give several reasons why you agree and one reason why you do not; 3) say "Thank you" to the person for getting you thinking; and 4) seek out her opinion on something else. In short, remember to agree even if agreement is just a starting point to an exchange of ideas.

Conclusion

When I say remember to agree, I don't mean agree for agreement's sake. Rather, utilize agreement as a way of building and continuing rapport with your child, avoiding unnecessary criticism, and putting the child in the right mindset for the balance of your communication. When we disagree with a child (intentionally or not), we tend to shut down communication and/or put the child in opposition to us. Then they spend all of their time and energy thinking about why they are right and we are wrong rather than how they might achieve something or continue to contribute to the family. Remember to begin by agreeing. Encourage critical thinking by eliciting information after agreement. Asking questions is one way of challenging our children to do better without being in opposition to them. Some good questions might include "What might happen if you did?" or "What would have to change in order for that to happen?" or "What tools or resources do you already have that could help you to do it?" and "What new tools or resources would you need?" All of these questions are beneficial and can be offered in an atmosphere of agreement.

Reminders and Actions

- Remember to agree first.
- Seek common ground before raising questions.
- Remember to use presuppositions.
- Become aware of your child's presuppositions.
- Remember to ask the person to use their imagination.
- To book David Frees as a speaker, for a seminar, or for a retreat call 1-800-769-5454 or visit Success Technologies' Web site, www.successtechnologies.com, for more information on David's programs.

Chapter

13

Get Them Thinking about Resources

"The greatest achievement of the human spirit is to live up to one's opportunities, and make the most of one's resources."

—Vauvenargves

A nother useful tool for improving communication is to ask children of all ages to identify the resources they would need in order to be able to perform some new or apparently daunting task. With older children this question can be asked more explicitly. For example, you could discuss the example of Apollo 13 where scientists made a list of the few items aboard the spacecraft and had to use only those items (luckily including duct tape) to solve all of the problems which threatened the crew members. If they failed, the crew would have perished. The creative use of resources can enhance and even save lives. With younger children we can get them thinking about resources metaphorically through stories. This technique is particularly useful where a child initially said "No," but now, thanks to presuppositions and the use of their imagination, is beginning to believe that he or she can or will be able to do it. At this point, you can reinforce this belief by saying, "Well, what would you have to have in order to do it?" "What kind of help would you need?" "What kind of tools?" "Would you need any money?" With a younger child you might ask them how a friend, a cartoon character, a kid from school, or their teacher might do it.

With kids of all ages you can make this a fun game and make it age-appropriate. For example, with teenage children you might ask, "How much money would you need to accomplish that?" "How could you do this if you didn't have any money?" "How could you solve this problem if all you had was a lemon and a cucumber?" With young children I might ask, "How would you do this with help from your pet or an imaginary pet?" "How could you do this with your brother?" "How about on your own?" I ask questions like these to get children to approach problem solving in a new way. It gets their creativity going and helps them to identify the resources they will need. They will begin to realize that "resources" are everywhere including previously unsuspected places. If they don't yet have the resources, questions can help them to develop a plan to get them.

Resources and actions are the tools we use to get from our current state to our desired state.

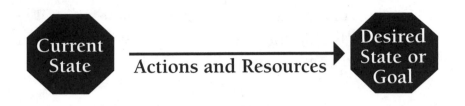

Children must learn that to move from imagination and desire, they must understand their resources *and* take action.

Generally, the more resources they realize are available to them the easier the task will seem and the less action will be required. For that reason, it is important to get children to become aware of what they need and to realize that they may already *have* many of the resources they need.

I sometimes suggest resources—like family members, teachers, cars, and their education (which they may not have even realized were resources).

By teaching children to recognize resources we teach them to find a way to achieve the desired goal that can be empowering, enjoyable, and satisfying. Often when children are beginning to stretch their goals, have received a challenging assignment, or you have made a suggestion to them that means moving beyond their comfort zone and their current abilities, they will need new resources in addition to those they already have. Good questioning will get them to realize and refine their goals, identify the resources they already have, and identify the resources they still need.

So you see this is really a five-step process. The first step is to utilize the techniques we have already reviewed in order to overcome objections. The second step is to have the child use his imagination to identify and refine the goal and then to work backward: "If you already have this thing that you want and you look back in time, how was it that you got here?" The third step is to get them to realize all of the resources they used in this imaginary exercise and to become aware of which of these they already have. This is a very empowering step; as much, if not all of what they need might already be within their grasp. If there are resources they need but do not yet have, the fourth step is now to get them to focus on how they might acquire those. You might ask them questions like: "How might you go about getting the ones you don't have, now?" "Who might have them?" "Why might they be willing to give them to you, lend them to you, or sell them to you?"

Finally, the fifth step is to take action. This requires motivation. All of the techniques in this book can be utilized to help children to understand, develop, and practice the self-discipline of motivating *themselves* and taking action. Pay attention to what really gets results. What tone of voice actually seems to get results. Notice what words create a positive response. Try this out on yourself. Which feels more motivating? "I must do this" or "I will do this" or "I have to do this." The words vary in their effect on us. Now repeat them again with a "sexy" tone of voice. Did one sentence or one tone of voice give you a greater sense of motivation? Just as certain words or tones of voice inspire you to action, your children will also have their own preferences. Become aware of them.

As with any technique, you have to be aware of how the

child is reacting. Remember, asking questions is a more discreet way of offering advice. If you offer advice or ask questions too often you may be rejected. As Adele Faber and Elaine Mazlish observe in their great book, *How to Talk so Kids Will Listen, and Listen so Kids Will Talk*, when you give advice to children, they, often feel stupid ("Why didn't I think of that?"), resentful ("Don't tell me how to run my life!"), or irritated ("What makes you think I didn't know that already?"). On the other hand, "When a child figures out for herself what she wants to do, she grows in confidence and is willing to assume responsibility for her decision." Clearly, questioning that inspires children is better than *advising*. Be aware of its effect and use it wisely to inspire children to recognize and seek out the resources they need.

Conclusion

Remember to ask questions, play games, and engage in activities that get the children in your life to focus on the resources they have and those they will need. Many times, children and adults believe that they cannot accomplish something because they do not have what it takes. By getting children to recognize that they have many, many resources which will help them on the way, they become more likely to imagine solutions using the resources they already have and more adept at spotting resources in their life for problem solving. Creating a mindset of abundance and resourcefulness is a powerful tool in communicating with children, solving problems, and generating solutions for yourself and others.

Reminders and Actions

- When you ask questions, make some of your questions outrageous. Remember to ask questions like, "How would you solve this problem if all you had was a grapefruit or a lemon?"
- Remember to create a mindset of abundance by having children recognize, repeat, and write down the many resources they have to solve a problem each time one comes up. By making problem solving and resource spotting a game we create resourceful, self-reliant children.
- Read *The Seven Powers of Questions*, and *Smart Questions* by Dorothy Leeds.
- Remember to make a note when a great question really works. Maybe you can use it again and again.

Chapter

14

Creating a Model
of Creativity

*"Out of abundance she took abundance
and abundance remains."*

—A sacred text *Upanishads*

As you can see from the examples throughout this book, creativity is one of the most useful and powerful tools of great communicators. When we encourage creativity and flexibility in ourselves we are no longer afraid of problems because we know that there are always options and solutions. When one attempted communication does not work the creative communicator realizes that there are many other strategies or tactics. There are many other ways to creatively solve our communication problems. The result—no fear.

There is an old adage that says when the only tool we have is a hammer then everything looks like a nail. When we have more creativity and confidence, we tend to say to ourselves, "Well, that didn't work that time, with this person. It may work in the future, even with this person, but I am going to move on to some other technique right now." Since we have lots of options we can simply try another way or another or another. There is no need to panic. In fact, being creative usually results in a sense of wealth, abundance, and confidence not only in communication but in all areas of our lives. Which seems more effective, the panicked parent, or the calm and resourceful parent? Which is the better role model? Remember to cultivate creativity.

Children who pay attention to the nonverbal stuff will notice that you are being creative. They will notice that you have tenacity and that you do not give up. They will model your creativity. They will model your tenacity. They will notice that you are without fear and model your demeanor. They will model your calm. They will notice that you have a sense of humor. That is better than simply disagreeing with them. That is better than arguing. So how do we become more creative?

Creativity is the source of all abundance. The economist Paul Pilzer describes the effect of creative thinking in his book *Unlimited Wealth*. According to Paul, there is no such thing as a limited resource. Each time we think we are running out of something, our creativity and technology find ways to create abundance out of scarcity.

Pilzer uses the example of computer technology. Only a short time ago in our history there was no computer industry. Then the silicon chip created trillions of dollars of wealth. All of that wealth developed from new ideas about how to use silicon (simple sand).

Albert Einstein also observed that creativity is more important than knowledge. So how do we tap into our enormous and unlimited wealth of creativity?

Becoming Happier and Much More Creative

In order to foster creativity in communication and to be fearlessly creative, I teach the following simplified problem solving and creativity model. My kids have stripped down a number of more complex problem solving models to these four steps known as **Ideas for F R E E.**™

1. **F**—Force yourself to keep going. Don't accept the first solution that comes to mind. Once you have stated your problem, keep going with the solutions. Usually, when we are faced with a problem or a question, our first solutions involve using the skills and information we most commonly use to solve problems. However, often the first few solutions we come up with are not the best, most elegant, and most creative. In fact, it is only when we force ourselves to keep going that we begin to combine and synthesize new and unusual skills, talents, ideas, and information.

It is through this combination of unusual information and ideas that we often develop our best and most creative thinking. When we combine multiple ideas into a new concept, it often has power and quality which exceeds some of the original ideas. For that reason, it is important to keep going. This also holds true in group and family communication. If a family is attempting to solve a problem through meetings or input from children, it is important that the family members all agree to keep going and to put as many ideas on the table as possible for later consideration.

One way to keep going is to say, "I will not stop creating solutions or ideas until I have 10, or 20, or 30." How do you keep getting ideas? Ask new questions. When you start to slow down, build your creative momentum by asking: "How could I solve this if I had millions of dollars? Or no money at all? How would I solve this if I were five years old or ninety-five years old?" Other provocative questions and systems include creating a solution beginning with each letter of the alphabet and asking yourself what would happen if you did just the opposite of each solution.

The point is, find ways to inspire your creativity and use them.

And remember, once you have expanded your mind in this way, it is a more powerful mind capable of even better solutions. Problem solving and creativity make us realize we are in a perpetual upward spiral.

2. **R**—Reserve judgment. When lots of strange ideas leap to mind the tendency is for us, whether alone or in a group, to begin to analyze and evaluate right away. We tend to say "No, that won't work." We begin to consider the various reasons why an idea will be ineffective. However, we want to reserve judgment. We want to get all of the crazy ideas on the table. Then and only then we may find that they are not so crazy and that there are ways to get them to work. However, when we are quick to criticize ourselves or others the "crazy" (or more creative) ideas are

never articulated. We miss the best and most innovative solutions. Criticism tends to be discouraging and to dampen creativity. At this point in the process reserve your criticism.

3. E—Evaluate. Now and only now is it time to review all of our ideas, and to decide which ones we can do with the time, resources, and energy available to us. When evaluating our own ideas or those of a group, there is a tendency to reject those ideas for which we intuitively sense we do not have the resources. However, if an idea is very resourceful, if it is exciting and offers an elegant solution or improvement it is usually worth the time to brainstorm the resource problem itself.

Let's say for example that a family meeting about a vacation resulted in a suggestion that the family should go to Australia. The reasons this trip would be great are many. It would be highly educational; it would be a wonderful experience; it would expose the children to exotic animals, the Great Barrier Reef, and lessons in geology, geography, and history. At first it seems that this idea is unworkable both because of the time it would take and the financial resources it calls for.

However, by brainstorming the issue of resources it may turn out that one parent could take a sabbatical and the other could make a long planned job change at the same time. That leaves, of course, the sticky question of financial resources. While the cost of this trip may at first seem daunting it might be possible to pool all of the family's frequent flyer or travel miles. Family members might forego holiday gifts, pool their money, or someone might take a part-time job. In short, there might be ways to acquire the resources necessary which do not, at first, seem obvious.

4. E—Enact. Action or implementation is a problem, even for people who go so far as to think things out. Make sure to draw up a long-term plan and to take some action toward the goal *right away*. When we start to act we build momentum. Even making a phone call, a note, or a reminder is movement in the right direction. It encourages us. This makes it more likely that we will continue to take action and build momentum.

The thing about taking action it is that there is often fear of failure. However, if by employing some of the techniques in this book we help to raise children who model our own creative problem solving behaviors rather than fear and who develop good habits, action will be less daunting to them. Furthermore, it is a good idea to examine our own motivation strategies. What is it that we are motivated to do? What do we say to ourselves? What images do we create? What consequences do we imagine if we act or fail to act? There are certain areas of our lives where most of us are highly motivated. We must explore this and note how it is that we go about developing motivation and momentum. It is also useful to begin to realize when it is that we lose motivation. In that way, we can interrupt the pattern we have developed of losing motivation at times and reenergize ourselves to continue to take action toward the things we want in life, toward the solution of our problems, and toward the achievement of the things we desire for ourselves and our family.

When we employ creative problem solving for ourselves as communicators and teach it to our children and the other recipients of our communications, we empower ourselves in ways many people fail to even imagine.

Conclusion

Just as it is important to raise children who are adept at spotting the resources they have available, it is also invaluable to teach children a *system* for being creative and for solving problems. It gives them a safety net. If problem solving does not happen spontaneously, they will have this system to fall back on. Problem solving essentially requires us to reserve judgment. The first step is to come up with as many solutions as possible to a particular problem, no matter how outrageous they may seem. Only later can we evaluate them given our resources, time, energy, and money. We also need to remind children that once the evaluation process is done it is necessary to develop and enact a plan for carrying them out and a fallback plan or plans in case Plan A fails.

Reminders and Actions

- When a child discovers problems or wants to develop new resources in their life, teach them to use the **Ideas for FREE**™ system. My own children have used their newly developed creative powers to create even better and better systems that work for them. However, this one is a good starting point and it's simple enough for me.
- Catch children being creative on their own and give them a prompt verbal reward, reminding them how powerful creativity can be.

- Become aware of how our society rewards creative people and the many ways in which creative people seem to develop a sense of abundance.
- Remember that creative people sometimes fail to notice or enjoy their own creativity and become despondent. Avoid despondency and celebrate creativity.

Chapter

15

Embedded
Suggestions

*"The greatest good you can do for another
is not just to share your riches, but to
reveal to him his own."*

—Prime Minister Benjamin Disraeli

Remember when I told you that some seminar audience members have accused me of teaching techniques that are "manipulative"? You may also remember that I said all communication is manipulation. You always want, either consciously or unconsciously, to get some result from your communication with others. It may not be a selfish result. It may be very altruistic. You may want to teach, encourage, or entertain. It is, however, all a type of manipulation. Your purpose in communication is what is important. Make sure that your purpose has a proper motivation. Of course, in this chapter, I am simply making explicit something that you already do. We all use embedded sugges-tions—we just don't realize it. Well this technique of embed-ded suggestions is very interesting and once you become con-sciously aware of it, it is likely to seem pretty manipulative. Remember, however, that you already do this much of the time. You do it unconsciously when you are communicating effectively. Now you can understand it, practice it, become more effective at it, and use it more responsibly.

The technique of using "embedded suggestions" comes from descriptions of Milton Erickson and those who fol-lowed Erickson in the area of medical hypnosis. Dr. Erickson was an interesting character and the father of modern therapeutic or medical hypnosis. Therapists would often give Erickson patients with whom they had had no luck over extended periods of time. Amazingly enough Erickson would spend a short time with the person and "suddenly" those patients would have new skills, new inter-ests, new abilities, and new effectiveness, and they were clearer about many of the things that they desired. Of course, embedded suggestions were not the only trick in Erickson's bag. He used many techniques. But for now let us **focus our attention** on the embedded suggestion.

I will describe how **embedded suggestions work**. Since you will not be able to hear my voice (unless you have an audio version of this book or a great imagination), I will use bold lettering to indicate where I have changed my tone, the speed or some other quality of my voice. Usually, I will emphasize the words of a suggestion a little. However, it is sometimes useful to whisper the embedded suggestions.

Remember how I explained that when talking to young children, it is a common mistake for a parent to say "Don't **forget to clean up your room.**" Go ahead. Say this to yourself and just emphasize the bold print ever so slightly. What came to your mind? How did that feel?

What you may find interesting about this sentence is that, as you know from the prior strategies section, children, when they hear this sentence, *must* make pictures of themselves forgetting to clean the room. Similarly, "Don't spill the milk" or "Don't talk to me that way" can make a young child nervous; can actually cause some physiological reaction such as trembling hands or they may immediately spill the milk. This unconscious embedded suggestion on the part of the parent emphasizes the behavior the parent wants to avoid. That is why it is in bold. Another example is when the teacher says "Don't **forget your homework.**" These are ways in which we may have used negative embedded suggestions or embedded commands. Generally, you want to **avoid negative** suggestions.

However, positive embedded suggestions can be very useful. For example, if we say "Remember to **do your homework**" or "**Be nice** to your sister, **now,**" our words may have a much more desirable effect. Repeat them to yourself and emphasize "do your homework" or "be nice to your sister, now"—but emphasize it with a tone consistent with intrigue and mystery. You are having the child imagine the desired result and getting the attention of the unconscious mind with the suggestion set off by your voice. The strange tone of voice catches their attention.

You can also call attention to a suggestion with hand signals. Have you ever used your hands to signal quotation marks around words you were speaking? This is another way to call attention to a suggested course of action. Imagine for a moment me speaking to you. I might say "I wonder if you are beginning to (**feel confident**) about your new skills." Assume that where I put the parentheses here I might actually change my voice and make a gesture with my hands so that I appear to "bracket" the words "feel confident." That is my suggestion to your unconscious mind. Does this seem silly? It is very serious. It works. Try it. Try enjoying embedded suggestions.

Would you like another powerful example of this technique? Have you ever had a conversation with a spouse or a child where you get to the end of the conversation, it stops, and they go on their way only to think of questions they wanted to ask you later? We can do something valuable here by using embedded suggestions. When I wrap up a conversation with a child, an adult, a client, or anyone, I try to remember to ask if there are any other questions. The problem with a general question like "Do you have any other questions?" is that the person may have them but not think of them until later. Or, they may have multiple questions but forget to ask you the most important ones. We always want to leave people with a sense of satisfaction or delight that they have spent time with us. If they had problems we hopefully helped to solve them. Let's see if we can improve the concluding questions.

You might try an alternative: "Is there any other question

you **need** to **ask me now** in order to feel completely sure that you understood everything I said and that you have gotten everything you need?"

Let's break this question down. "Is there any other question you need to ask me now in order to feel completely sure of _____?" (insert here whatever it is that you want)

1. How many questions do I want? The sentence indicates that I want only one question. Given the rest of the sentence, this will produce an efficiency. It will force the other person to search whatever remaining questions they have in their mind to find the one that is most important to them.

2. When do I want them to ask me the question? Notice that that there is an embedded suggestion to "**ask me now.**" I also set this up using my voice and moving my head and sometimes I bracket it with my hand. In other words, when I am saying "**ask me now**" I also put parentheses around it. The unconscious part of your mind says "Hey, what was that? That looked like parentheses around . . . oh, '**ask me now.**' " They will ask you right then and there. You might find this surprising but you already do this when you communicate eloquently. Notice when you get the results you want, and you will begin to catch yourself embedding suggestions. You will realize how effective it has always been and that it can be even more effective for you now.

3. Notice that I said, "is there any other question which if you ask it now" will make you feel a certain way. I am actually asking for a question which will trigger the

desired feeling in the person I am talking to. In this case, the feeling that they understand the communicator. This is very important whenever you conclude a conversation. You can either leave the conversation with the person feeling confused, completely satisfied, or somewhere in between. In this case, I am making a suggestion that if they should search their mind and ask a question. But, I am also suggesting that they look for a question which, if they ask it, will make them feel better. The act of asking that question triggers positive feelings.

What is interesting about this question is that you will usually get one of two responses. People will move their eyes around through space looking for a question that will make them feel the suggested way.

After that, they will answer in one of two ways. They may answer emphatically "No!" This simply means that your communications were clear and they don't need to ask any questions. They understand and they already feel that they understand.

Or, they will say "Yes!" and they ask a question. This question, because of the way you have asked your own question, will create a feeling of satisfaction or some other desirable feeling and can provide you with a lot of additional information. In this way you avoid the problem of the child, the spouse, or whomever leaving and having questions occur to them later which were really essential to the effectiveness of the communication. You want those questions now—while you can still deal with them.

Increasingly, parents and college-age and adult children

are communicating by e-mail. Embedded suggestions, as we have discussed them, seem to apply to face-to-face communication. However, if you look at this chapter, and through the book you will notice a number of embedded suggestions set off in bold print. You can use such suggestions in e-mail. However, use them sparingly and with a sense of humor. The less bold and the more discreet the font change the better. However, this avoids the central issue. Be sure not to rely upon e-mail exclusively.[21] Make time for phone calls and visits to adult children and make more time in your life for young children and grandchildren. There is no substitute for spending time with them.

Conclusion

There is infinite wealth and abundance within each of us. If you want to make your communication with your children or your spouse or partner rich, abundant, elegant, and simple, then it is worth the time to practice. Practice, however, can either be drudgery or it can be fun. It is up to you to choose. You can approach these things and do them in a way that produces enjoyment or do them in a way that seems hard. Remember the reticular activating system and that you get what you look for. Ask yourself exciting and motivating questions. "How can I become a better communicator so that my children can feel, understand, and know my love?" "How can I do this in a way that makes them more likely to succeed in school and helps them become the best people they possibly can?" Then the parent, the spouse, or grandparent within you will be highly motivated by the answers you get.

Reminders and Actions

- Understand embedded suggestions.
- Begin to recognize that **you already use them**.
- Practice using a tone of voice that suggests fun, mystery, or intrigue.
- Bear in mind that you can call attention to a suggestion with physical gestures, tone of voice, change of inflection, or change of speed.
- Embedded suggestions can circumvent resistance and help others to realize their own potential.

NOTE: For more information on the use of embedded commands or suggestions read: *My Voice Will Go with You*, by Milton Erickson and *Tranceformations*, by Bandler and Grinder. These titles are available through many bookstores, and at www.successtechnologies.com. Remember to register and download the NLP/Hypnosis Bibliography.

Chapter

16

Using Tag Questions Is Good, Isn't It?

"The first key to wisdom is this—constant and frequent questioning..."

—Peter Abelard, 1120

Questions are one of the most powerful tools of effective communication. They stimulate thinking and help guide focus. They can spark creativity and lead us to information we might never otherwise get. Great leaders use questions rather than direct orders. Questions can be persuasive because they do not impose our view but allow others to discover and convince themselves. Tag questions in particular give parents a tool to help a child review what the parent has said. They give us a chance to understand the conclusions the child has reached without demanding a detailed review of reasoning by the child. They give us a chance to stimulate a child's creativity and to guide it without imposing our own view. A tag question is simply a question offered quickly and nonchalantly at the end of a statement or observation, which encourages review of the previous communication. Tag questions also help children to see the value of questioning and to build good habits of communication.

For example, when a child has been experiencing difficulties and has shown some improvement you may observe to the child, "Wow, I'll bet that seemed better to you in a number of ways. Didn't it?" You have not told them *your* view of the specific ways. You have not put the focus on you or your feelings. You have left it up to the child to think about it. Tag questions are frequently treated as rhetorical questions. They often seem, when delivered with the correct nonchalant tone, to require no answer. However, tag questions have the effect of encouraging the listener to review what went on and in this case the ways in which the child improved.

Another example would be where a child is having difficulty with vocabulary in school. In that case, the parent might say "It seems that you might want to forget about the distractions. Don't you?" or "You can find a better and easier way to memorize the words **now**. Can't you?" Questions, like this encourage the child to use his or her own creativity and evaluate the suggestion. The statement is a suggestion by the parent but the heavy lifting, the thinking and problem solving, is left to the child.

Tag questions can also be used very effectively in conjunction with embedded suggestions, which we examined in the previous chapter. For example, when a parent uses an embedded suggestion by saying "Remember to **ask good questions** in school." They have given the unconscious mind a suggestion to **ask good questions**. Tag questions might improve this by saying "Remember to ask good questions today in school. Won't you?" This type of tag question offers the child the opportunity to say yes or to say no. If they answer out loud you will receive information you might otherwise never have gotten. The child may say "Okay, I will." If they seem genuine, excited, and motivated then they have formed a partnership with you and agreed to ask good questions and it becomes more likely that they will. They may say "No, I won't." If they say no we can use some of the other techniques we examined earlier to deal with refusal. At an appropriate time, you can ask what has to happen in order for them to feel comfortable doing it. You might ask, "Can you imagine any way in which asking questions would be beneficial to you?" or "Fun for you?" "Can you come up with other ways to learn?"

However, the child may not actually answer out loud. In this case, you do not know for sure whether they have refused or assented to your suggestion from the language of their response because they have not responded with language. However, be aware of their physiology, tone of voice, and other factors. These clues will give some hint of their internal evaluation of your suggestion. Over time, you can continue to work with the child until you find a suggestion with which they do agree, or which enthralls or excites them.

Conclusion

Asking questions offers us the opportunity to review our suggestions with our children and to examine their reactions. When we ask questions and then listen, we are encouraging our children to review and evaluate what they have heard and to store their thinking. We are helping them to build a good habit of communication and helping them to develop the skill of asking good questions.

Reminders and Actions

- Remember to use tag questions from time to time, won't you?
- Tag questions can be used effectively in conjunction with embedded commands. An embedded suggestion or command might be "Remember to ask good questions in school." The same embedded suggestion with a tag question is "Remember to ask good questions in school today, won't you?" "You play well. Don't you?" "You can **learn that now**. Can't you?"
- Always listen to and watch the child's reaction. Do not overuse any technique. What works with one child will not always work with another and what worked one day may not work the next.
- Be flexible in your approach.
- Great questions inspire great answers. Spend some time each day thinking of great questions for your kids.

17

The Power of a
Sense of Humor

*"That is the saving grace of humor—if you
fail, no one is laughing at you."*

—Comedian A. Whitney Brown

There are clearly times as a parent when we need to be stern. More often than not, however, there are humorous aspects to the interactions with our family members that warrant our attention. Often, we have decided to be stern when we do not need to be. Often, we have decided to ignore the humor or to deny it and play out some preconceived parental role. The truth is, however, that as human beings we love humor. We love to feel the enjoyment and sheer pleasure in life that is created by humor. Children of all ages are fans of laughter or simply that warm feeling that comes from sharing humor with their parent. Yet, how often do we enjoy giving them that gift? Would you like to do it more often? Many people report that at work they are considered to be jovial, filled with endless and boundless energy, and happy—only to find themselves feeling stressed and despondent at home. They frequently find themselves devoid of humor even when it is desirable. Make a commitment *now* to finding the humor in the parent/child relationship and then sharing it with your child. You may be surprised at the immediate rapport and bond that results and that your other communication skills become more elegant and effective as well.

Often, children and adults find a suggestion delivered in a humorous story or through a metaphor is much more powerful than a direct order. Again, they do not feel that their behavior has been directly confronted. Rather they have been offered an alternative, in a way that was amusing and which made them laugh. In fact, your requests may become associated, in their minds, with a feeling of happiness rather than anger or distress. The respect for the parent who is delivering that message or alternative is heightened, the enjoyment of receiving the message is improved, and the likelihood the child will consider and enact the suggested behavior is increased. Let's take an example. Dottie Walters is a national treasure—a mother, well-known international speaker, the founder of multiple businesses and of the speaker's association IGAB. She related a story to me once that illustrates the power of humor.

Dottie found herself frustrated day after day when the children (whose responsibility it was to pack their lunch each morning before school) would not get up on time to ready themselves and pack their lunches before the bus came. One day Dottie found herself becoming more and more concerned about this behavior. However, as so many ingenious parents do, she caught herself becoming annoyed and simply shook her head. She interrupted her annoyance.[22] She realized that this was a silly situation that required a silly response.

As a busy mom, Dottie knew that the children might shirk their responsibility and come to expect her to make the lunches. However, by her own admission, her cooking skills were infamous and she did not bring a lot of creativity and greatness to the luncheon menu. Her strategy was to help her kids develop the good habits of being early risers and getting their lunches together and completing their chores. So, knowing that the kids did not really like her lunches she knocked on everyone's door one morning and told them to hurry up or she would pack their lunch for them for the next week. In this way, she made her help seem like a punishment. Her children were entertained, and in the end, she told me, one of her children, who laughed so hard that morning, became a well-known chef.

Rather than angrily confronting children who have misbehaved, made a bad choice, or failed to carefully consider alternative behaviors that might be more effective, try more palatable and successful techniques like humor, storytelling, and metaphors.

Of course this is a two-way street. It is also important to be on the lookout for humor expressed by children or other family members. There are probably many times in our lives where we have overlooked a smile, a joke, or an attempt at humor that would have amused us if we had given it a chance. When a child is amused by her parents (at almost any age), the relationship improves and the opportunity for deeper communication is enhanced.

There are numerous additional strategies and tactics for effective communication. The purpose of this book is to give you insight into the ones that are the most essential, refined, and powerful, the ones most likely to produce dramatic and useful results quickly. For that reason, I have kept the number of strategies and tactics to a minimum so that you can appreciate them, practice them, use them, and find them delightful. For more information about strategies and tactics and about communication in general you can visit our Web site or look for future books in this series.

Conclusion

It is the nature of our biochemistry that when we smile and when we see happiness, our outlook on the world changes for the better. In fact, there is a rich body of scientific and inspirational literature that examines the value of humor in healing, in enhancing life, and in communication. Numerous articles have been written studying the release of neurotransmitters when we laugh and the effects of these on our bodies and our outlooks on life. You don't have to search this literature and you don't have to take my word for it. Just experiment and try amusing your children. Try noticing when they amuse you. Enjoy the opportunities for deeper, more pleasurable communication that occur naturally when life is more pleasurable.

Reminders and Actions

- Tell an age-appropriate joke, riddle, pun, or humorous story to your child each day.
- Ask them to tell you one.
- Make it a habit to relate amusing stories or experiences.
- If something funny or embarrassing happens, be willing to share it with your children and let them see that you find it amusing.
- Remember to find it amusing.

The End as the Beginning

"Knowing is not enough, we must apply.
Willing is not enough, we must do."

—Artist and Scientist Johann von Goethe

Knowing what to do is not enough. As parents, we must take action. We must parent in the best way that we know how. Yet, what works one day may not work the next. What works with one child may not with another. Parenting, it turns out, is a complex bit of business. So, if we want to enjoy parenting and life, we have to enjoy being flexible, adapting and taking action.

You would not have picked up this book, turned it over, looked at it and purchased it if you had not been interested in improving your life and the life of your child. One of the ways to make a profound difference and improvement in a child's life is by understanding how to communicate more effectively, and then to apply that knowledge.

This book is a review of some of the most profound principles and techniques of communication. I am sure, as you read through the book, you began to realize that when you are communicating powerfully and effectively with your children or family members, you are *already* doing many of these things. However, by becoming aware of the principles and tactics of great communication skills, and of your own great communication skills, you improve the likelihood that you can do even better more often. Would it be worth the time you spent reading this book if you could improve your relationship with your children by even the tiniest fraction? And what if you could make even more dramatic long-term changes?

So now, as you reach the end of the book, you begin the process of making changes. As you do it, it is worth a few more moments to review the central concepts of improving communication. If you need more motivation, remember that great communication helps to build healthy, happy and self-reliant children. So where to begin?

Great parenting first requires you to understand that you need to create an opportunity for your children to grow and to become the best communicators and problem solvers, and the most caring and compassionate people that they can be. This requires that you set limits for them so that they have a safe place in which to grow and develop. It requires, as time goes on, that you give them more and more responsibility and that you have age-appropriate expectations for them.

Effective communication skills can make all of this easier. First and foremost, to be a great communicator you need to develop flexibility. Flexibility allows you to examine your beliefs about communication and to adopt and act on those new beliefs that make your communication with your family members and children more effective. By cultivating your flexibility, you can learn to adopt the beliefs that improve your skills. You can choose to reject the beliefs that no longer serve you.

Another principle which has the capacity to produce a massive and effective change in how you communicate is the realization that great communicators develop their sensory acuity, or attention to detail. They become aware of the fact that words alone do not have the same meaning to each person. They become aware that every individual and every child processes language in a unique way, and in a way that is different from your own. Great communicators watch and listen attentively to their children when they communicate. They use language, gestures and tone of voice to confirm to their children that they are listening. And they create the time to listen in family rituals that allow children time to speak.

Great communicators are fascinated by the complex and diverse range of human behavior and communication, and they tend to find the humor in as much as possible. They practice feeling good for no reason at all. Think about it. Having a pleasant countenance, being happy and finding enjoyment in life is not an abnegation of a parent's responsibility. There are times when it is appropriate to be stern with children, but, for the most part, effective communicators and effective parents create a loving environment in which their children can learn by remembering to find the humor in an event and remembering to feel good.

Feeling good also helps us to make better decisions. Can you remember a time when you were angry, frustrated, or distraught and made some of the best decisions in your life? No? It is more probable you made the best decisions in your life when you were well rested, when you smiled, when you felt good and when you could bring your good judgment to bear.

Great family communicators also remember to make their communication outcome-based. If you need your children to do something, or want your children to do something, then it is important for you to have an understanding of that goal *before* you begin to communicate with your children. If you are concerned about a teenage child's exposure to drugs, alcohol or other dangers in their lives you will be a much less effective communicator if you have not thought out your concern and the behavior you desire from your teen before you begin to communicate with them.

Great communicators and great parents have a plan. They figure out, at the big-picture level, how they would like to raise their children. They have a plan. However, great communicators never mistake the plan for reality. Planning simply makes us unafraid to proceed in life and to have a great time raising our children. Rare, indeed, is the plan that actually works out. That brings us back to flexibility. By planning, we have the knowledge that allows us to be flexible, to enjoy life and keep going no matter how difficult life or parenting becomes.

Once you recognize the big principles that underlie all effective communications, it's then useful to understand and practice some of the techniques, practices and tools that other effective communicators use in their lives. This book is packed with brilliant little tools for more effective communication. I do not take credit for discovering these tools. I do not take credit for refining them. I have found references to these tools from the earliest times in the Bible, to the most recent studies in psychology, neuroscience, and linguistics. I have tried to express them in a way that makes them interesting and accessible.

Do they work? Yes. They all work, but not all of the time. Will you find them all comfortable to use? Maybe. Maybe not. It is likely that you will be comfortable using many of these throughout your life. However, by knowing about them, by practicing them, by employing them and by finding out when they work, you become more comfortable and more flexible.

There is an old adage that when the only tool you have is a hammer, then every problem looks like a nail. This book was designed to fill your toolbox with techniques for great and effective communication so that you don't have to use anger, yelling or the same old tools.

The flexible communicator feels comfortable. If one technique fails, they realize that particular technique just failed at that time with that person. The effective communicator does not throw the technique away. They simply keep it for another time when they feel that it will be appropriate. However, they do not get angry, frustrated or become afraid. There is always another technique to try.

Some of the most interesting and powerful techniques are worth, not only a quick review but a note to begin to use them. Knowing them is not enough. Having the courage to try them, to be fascinated by them, and to enjoy using them is the key. For example, the effective communicator and great parent realizes that they need to build rapport in conversation whether it is with a young child, teenager or an adult child. Your wisdom, suggestions, rules or other information that you wish to convey is always going to be better received when the person to whom you are speaking feels comfortable with you, likes and respects you, and is interested in what you have to say.

Truly effective communicators try to avoid negation. It seems natural that we are always telling our children not to spill their soda and telling our teenage children, "Don't drink." The problem is that, because of the way in which the human mind processes language, we are having our young children, teenage children and adult children mentally rehearse the very behaviors we wish them to avoid. Remember, instead, to avoid negation and to use language in a way that helps your children mentally rehearse the behavior you desire.

Great communicators remember to tailor their communication to the individual.

They realize that each and every child has a different way of processing language. They watch and listen for clues as to what children are doing and try to adapt their own communication to appeal to that child.

Great communicators also use presuppositions to expand their children's minds and their thoughts of what they are capable of accomplishing. The parent remembers to agree with the child and acknowledges the child's feeling while allowing the child to begin to believe in himself.

Effective communicators and parents play games with their children and use real-life examples to get their children thinking about the resources that are available to them, and to help their children build great problem-solving tools. If we, as parents, always solve our children's problems for them, we raise children who are dependent. When we support our children, but allow them to use their minds creatively, we raise their self-esteem and we allow them to become more effective children and, later, adults. In essence, we help them to develop the traits of confidence and flexibility by modeling our own effective behavior.

Great communicators make it a point to listen carefully. They create opportunities for their children to talk, and they realize that children need time to broach the most important topics.

As I said, the conclusion is only the beginning. As a second-degree black belt and a martial arts teacher for years, I have been telling children as they advance and achieve a black belt, that the black belt is only the beginning. Children are sometimes shocked to realize that after four or five years of training they have only now reached the point where they know that there is so much that they do not yet know. In his book, *Mastery*, George Leonard reminds the reader that those people that achieve mastery in anything are the ones that allow themselves to enjoy the process of learning. In anything that we do we practice, practice, practice and almost always have a sudden burst of improvement. However, we often practice for long periods of time without seeing any major results. The people who achieve mastery enjoy the long periods of practice, as well as bursts of improvement.

In this case, though, the goals of having healthy, happier children and families, of overcoming adversity in our family relationships and of being the best parents that we can be are so motivating and compelling that I am sure you can find plenty of happiness along the way. Begin to take action. Commit now to doing something—anything—that caught your eye, that sounds good, that seems compelling. Take action and enjoy the results.

Develop your own techniques, find what works for you and remember to be flexible and to practice feeling good for any reason, or for no reason at all. Your children will thank you.

A Thought for Parents

Go placidly amid the noise and the haste, and remember what peace there may be in silence. As far as possible, without surrender, be on good terms with all persons. Speak your truth quietly and clearly, and listen to others, even the dull and ignorant; they too have their story . . . be yourself. Especially, do not feign affection. Neither be cynical about love; for in the face of all aridity and disenchantment, it is as perennial as the grass. Take kindly the counsel of the years, gracefully surrendering the things of youth. Nurture strength of spirit to shield you in sudden misfortune. But do not distress yourself with imaginings. Many fears are born of fatigue and loneliness. Beyond a wholesome discipline, be gentle with yourself. You are a child of the universe no less than the trees and the stars; you have a right to be here. And whether or not it is clear to you, no doubt the universe is unfolding as it should. Therefore, be at peace with God, whatever you conceive Him to be; and whatever your labors and aspirations in the noisy confusion of life, keep peace with your soul. With all of its sham, drudgery and broken dreams, it is still a beautiful world.

—Max Ehrmann

Part Four

Frequently Asked Questions,
Resources and Appendices

"Success is going from failure to failure without loss of enthusiasm."

—Prime Minister Winston Churchill

Introduction to Appendices

As this book developed, parents, friends, editors, seminar participants, and others read it. For each reader it would inspire different questions. The questions always involved how best to apply these strategies and tactics to the reader's particular family situation. While no single book can anticipate all of the situations that might arise, everyone agreed that it would be useful to consider some of the most commonly asked questions, and to provide some world-class examples of successful communication.

For that reason, the following appendices will consider questions and situations which fall into several broad categories. Those categories include questions posed by new and expectant parents, parents of early verbal children, parents of young school-aged children, parents of teenage children, and questions posed by the parents of adult children.

The answers to these questions are not meant to be exhaustive, but merely to illustrate possible solutions and to get you thinking about how you might handle these situations if they were to arise in your own family. As you read these, consider if the solution chosen by the parent in the story would have been appropriate for you. Pay particular attention to how the answer relates to the strategies of great communication such as congruency and making communication outcome-based. Also notice how specific tactics such as humor, embedded suggestions, avoiding negation, and using agreement and silence all help to achieve the desired result.

1

Frequently Asked Questions by Expectant and New Parents

"The joyfulness of a man prolongeth his days."

—Psalms

1. "Does singing, playing music, or communicating with my baby in utero help the baby's development?"

My own view on this question is that it could not hurt, and if it makes you feel better, you should do it. For a more scientific analysis, I turned to Dr. Fred Wirth, the author of *Prenatal Parenting*. Dr. Wirth's mission is no less than the elimination of youth violence by helping parents understand the prenatal effects of stress on the unborn, and how those effects can continue into life. Dr. Wirth's excellent book, *Prenatal Parenting*, is available at our Web site www.successtechnologies.com, and Dr. Wirth's book and other products are available through his Web site www.prenatalparenting.com. Dr. Wirth's conclusions are also supported by an extensive body of work by Western scientists which is examined in Daniel Goleman's book, *Destructive Emotions*.

Dr. Wirth advocates a number of stress-reduction techniques which involve taking three moments out of each day (he calls them "Fetal Love Breaks"™) to express your love for your unborn child in a quiet way. These stress-reduction techniques help to create an in utero environment conducive to positive brain development which, according to Dr. Wirth, "will help families birth happy, healthier babies with peaceful minds."

Since verbally communicating with your child or creating an atmosphere involving music or sound is soothing to *you*, it also has a positive effect on your unborn child. It produces a physiological state that benefits your baby and is absolutely worth pursuing. Dr. Wirth suggests that this alone may help us to have healthier, better-adjusted children. He tells us that, in this way, parents "help to build world peace one baby at a time."

2. "You said that the words we select make up only a small part (7%) of communication. What other factors make up the other 93% of communication? Are there other things I should be doing with my newborn child in addition to speaking to him or her?"

The answer is an emphatic "yes." However, while body language, tone and speed of speech, and other factors make up much of our communication, words are important. They are especially important to children. In short, you should speak to your newborn child constantly. Newborn and growing children will love the sound of your voice and they will be learning important pre-verbal skills that lead to speech recognition and verbal skills. The next thing to consider, whenever medically possible, is breastfeeding your child. Robin Frees, IBCLC, a certified lactation consultant, tells us that scientific studies have shown that nursing is statistically linked with higher IQ and with the reduction of childhood allergies, upper respiratory infections, and ear infections. Robin can be reached at www.newbornconcepts.com or rbfibclc@aol.com. Robin has worked with thousands of mothers, physicians, nurses, and lactation consultants and she anecdotally observes that nursing a child creates an opportunity for physical bonding, comforts the baby, and allows quiet time for mother and child to be together during this unique developmental stage. Since your newborn child is preverbal, one of the best ways you can show your affection for the child is to engage in physical cuddling and contact.

While there are advocates of allowing newborn children to cry, and of denying them physical contact as a way of creating habits of discipline, the general scientific consensus is that young children cannot be spoiled. Rather, preverbal children should be comforted when they cry. This will create children who thrive from this contact and feel secure and welcomed in their new world.

In fact, Dr. Wirth is emphatic on this issue. According to

Dr. Wirth, the primary goal of a newborn child is to establish a relationship with an adult. Newborns will expend enormous amounts of energy experimenting with their environment to discover what works. According to Dr. Wirth, if babies are held only when they cry, then they will cry for attention. However, when they receive attention for positive behaviors unassociated with crying this attention reinforces those other behaviors and the babies tend to be healthier and happier. Furthermore, Dr. Wirth states that if children are ignored or denied contact their "brain development begins to collapse."

To support this, Dr. Wirth's book, *Prenatal Parenting*, cites a 1940 study of institutionalized children in which their high mortality rate was linked to the small amount of time spent with adults.

3. "What are the advantages of interacting with, and speaking to, young children even when they are preverbal?"

By speaking to your children, reading to them, and singing to them, you are providing the foundation of their understanding of human language. You are giving the young child neurological stimulation which helps the child sort out and understand the sounds and environment around him. Children of all ages enjoy hearing stories. For that reason alone, reading to a child should be considered from the earliest ages. Remember to use various inflections and tones of voice when speaking to your child, reading to your child, and telling stories or singing. In this way, according to Dr. Wirth, you help to develop your child's verbal and emotional IQ. In fact, Dr. Wirth tells us that newborn children have greater auditory acuity at three weeks of age than at three years of age. They are able to identify their mother's face and to distinguish it from similar faces within hours of birth. They are learning machines, equipped from the earliest moments to learn.

Because their senses are so keen, soothing inflection is also important to young children. From their very earliest moments following birth babies enjoy hearing their parents' voices and variations of tone, including excitement, intrigue and other emotional states expressed through voice and gesture. This eventually helps the child link tone and other qualities of voice to meaning.

Remember, also, to be a good model for your children. If, from the very start when they are watching your behavior, you exhibit anxiety and concern at the slightest provocation, they will sense that anxiety and will begin to produce neurotransmitters of fear and alarm when they might not otherwise be appropriate. By contrast, if you cultivate calm states, learning states, and playful states, the child will mimic your physiology and produce neurotransmitters associated with those positive physical states.

Many scientific studies support the idea that the first few years of life are one of the most important periods of brain development. It is especially important in developing the ability to avoid negative, destructive emotions. Dr. Wirth and others advocate exercises designed to make connections between the emotional center of the brain associated with anger and violence (the amygdala) and the frontal cortex (which allows us to consider and reflect upon our actions rather than acting them out immediately). All of the evidence suggests that the time we spend helping our newborn and preverbal children to make those connections may be one of the most important things we do as parents.

4. "How can I help to instill an inquisitive mind in my newborn?"

Historically, in indigenous societies children were exposed to their parents', and grandparents', work, interactions, and behaviors all day long. They learned from their parents, or other adults, throughout the day. In more recent times, there has been a separation of children and their parents. Because one or more parent has gone to work, children are not able to view their parents' communication, interaction, and behavior over extended periods of time. They are not able to view their parents', or other adults', reactions to a variety of situations and interactions that historically they had observed. There is also a tendency in our society to shelter children from the outside world for an extended period of time after birth. However, taking your child with you, in whatever activity, permits the child from a very early age to sense your emotions, observe your actions and reactions, and, in all likelihood, to develop a more diverse understanding of the world. Make your children an active part of your life.

As parents, and as a society, we face some hard questions about our work lives and personal practices, and the effects they have on our children. Have your child with you as often as you can—shop with him, travel with him, play with him, and read to him. Whenever possible, draw, sing, build and encourage him in activities which utilize different skills. When your work does not permit this, use your remaining time with your child wisely. Do not worry too much about the type of activity. Just be with your child.

Appendix

2

Frequently Asked Questions about Preschool and School-Age Children

"My mother said to me, 'If you become a soldier, you'll be a general; if you become a monk, you'll end up the Pope.' Instead, I became a painter and wound up as Picasso."

—Artist Pablo Picasso

1. "How do I stimulate my preschool child to become an inquisitive and natural learner?"

   Parents can help to create a love of learning in their children. First, realize that there are many styles of learning. Not all children learn about the world in the same way and not all children enjoy the same activities as a way of learning. Having said that, one of the best ways to create a love of learning in preschool and school-age children is to engage in storytelling and reading as part of a family ritual. Storytelling and reading, when done optimally, have the advantage of requiring the child to interact with the reader or storyteller. They are interacting with you—their parent. Those activities require the direct application of the child's imagination. They are active, not passive. Of course, your use of voices, physical gestures, facial expressions, voice tones, and drama helps to stimulate and involve more of the child's brain.

By making storytelling and reading habitual, and by involving your child in the activity, you encourage the habit of using her mind creatively. You can also be a model for your children by allowing them to see you reading on your own.

Involving your children in reading and storytelling can be hilarious for you and for them. For example, asking them what they think will happen next is a great way of involving them.[23]

Or, as you tell a story, ask them to take over and tell the next part. If they are reluctant, have them fill in a word or two. They will begin to feel creative and you may hear some of the funniest stories.

The second way you can stimulate the minds of young children is by the intelligent use of questions. There is a tendency when children come home from school to ask them, "What happened today?" Frequently, though the child may have been gone for a six- to eight-hour period, he answers

"Nothing." That "nothing" occurred for eight hours is, in my experience, unlikely. During that much time, something almost always happens. A common parental reaction to this statement is often to say, "Of course something happened!" This places you, the parent, in a posture of disagreement with your child. It may seem like an innocent disagreement, but it is a disagreement nonetheless. While parent/child disagreements are inevitable, and in some cases healthy, I prefer to experience them only when necessary. Rather, I like to ask questions which engage the child's imagination. For example, I will ask, "What was the most bizarre, unusual, or dramatic thing that happened today?" I might also ask "Did you ask any great questions today?" Or I might say, "Okay. If something bad happened—what was it?"

These questions have a very different effect on a child and on your relationship with the child. Even if the child chooses not to answer you, he cannot help but review the day while looking for those things. Remember when we experimented with the statement, "Don't think of the color blue!" When I say, "Don't think of the color blue!" your immediate reaction is to think of the color blue. You can't understand my question without seeing the color blue and then negating it. Likewise, when you ask a child, "What was the most interesting, fascinating, or delightful thing that happened to you in school today?" he may not choose to answer you audibly, but he *will* review the day and make note of those things. Even if the child says nothing, the question is a more useful one because of this. You have engaged his mind and you are not in disagreement with the child.

I tend to use questions like this in a habitual way. For a week or more I may ask the same question. One of my children's teachers asked me at a parent/teacher conference, "What was that exchange between Josh and Jamie that happened in the hallway the other day? Joshua passed Jamie and he said to her, 'Did you get it yet, did you get it?' and she responded 'No, I didn't, but you know he is going to ask.'" I smiled because the question I had been asking them was "What was the most interesting thing that happened at school today?"

My two children, in first and third grades respectively, were walking around the halls, sitting in class, eating lunch, and playing on the playground at one level, yet always looking for the most interesting thing that was going to happen to them that day. That is an exciting environment in which to attend school. Both of those children are excellent students and seem to enjoy school immensely. Do they have difficult days? Do they have trouble with friends? Yes. Occasionally, they have the same problems and dilemmas that all students have.

However, on a day-to-day basis they seem to be fascinated by school, enjoy school, and love going to school.

2. "How do you deal with a child who refuses to live up to your perception of his or her potential?"

Parents and seminar participants frequently ask me how to deal with refusal by a child. They feel that they are encouraging their child, but the child simply refuses and says, "I can't do that." The natural tendency of parents when faced with a refusal is to attempt to encourage the child by saying, "Yes you can—I know that you can do it." That, however, is really the rub. It is the *parent* who knows, and not the child. The parent believes in the child, but the child doesn't yet believe in him or herself. Furthermore, by attempting to be a supportive parent we have placed ourselves in opposition to the child. The child says that they cannot. We say that they can. When we say this, the child's natural tendency is to make a list, either in her mind or verbally, of all of the reasons why you are wrong and she is right. They list the reasons why they can't do something. This doesn't help—it is likely to emphasize the block rather than eliminate it.

Instead, consider using agreement to your advantage. A better response is to say, "I know that you feel you can't do it yet." This acknowledges the child's feelings and suggests (albeit discreetly) that she may be able to do the activity in the future. You are not disagreeing with the child—you are actually agreeing with her. A barrier to further communication has been avoided. At that point, if you are simply quiet and leave a moment of silence she may recognize your agreement with her. She may think about it and begin to describe what would have to happen in order for her to be able to do it. If the moment of silence continues, you may offer such a suggestion through another question. You may ask, "What would have to happen in order for you to be able to do it now?" or "What would happen, and how would you feel, if you could do it now?" Again, there is no disagreement; you are simply asking the child to use his or her imagination. Using imagination is much easier than trying to believe that she can do it.

If, by using some of the suggestions in the previous chapters, you have helped to raise a child with a fertile imagination, he or she will love the project that you have discreetly assigned (i.e. developing a list of what is needed, or what has to happen, in order for them to be able to do it). Again, remember that even if the child does not respond, she cannot help but engage in this imaginary activity in order to understand your question.

3. "How do you handle a young child who behaves rudely?"

Rude behavior is a value judgment. What is rude behavior in one household may not be viewed that way in another. However, you are the parent. You set the standard. So when you view unacceptable behavior, realize that rude behavior probably has its origin in one of two sources. The first possibility is that the child may be modeling your own behavior. Alternatively, the child may be deliberately resisting your definition of appropriate behavior.

In the first instance, the child may see you behaving in a particular way and may be reproducing your behavior in the same context. Or they may see you behaving in a way that is not rude in one context, but is rude in another. If you have unconsciously set an example of rude behavior, you need to become aware of your own behavior and begin to change it so that it is appropriate. If, however, the child is exhibiting a behavior that is appropriate in one context but not another, you must educate him. You have to say that he may have seen you acting that way, but that in some places that behavior is okay and not in others. For example, a young child may experience the thrill and exhilaration of playing in a park, but not yet understand that racing around or raising his voice is not appropriate in a restaurant.

Of course, teaching these lessons requires language that is age-appropriate. The child must be at an age where he can understand the distinctions we are trying to make.

Consistency in your own behavior is especially important here. If we want children to understand that they can't run around in a restaurant, that rule may need to be taught consistently from the earliest time in *all* restaurants. It is hard for some children to understand that they can run around in a fast food restaurant, but not in another restaurant. It may be better to teach, initially, that a restaurant is a restaurant, and that your expectations of behavior are specific. As children become older, more refined distinctions come naturally. Again, it may be useful to use some of the other tools we have discussed. You may, for example, ask them a question. "Can you tell me why it is important for you to stay calm in a restaurant?" "Can you tell me how you would feel if you wanted it to be quiet, but somebody else was making a lot of noise?"

Have the child use her imagination to come to an understanding of her own. If a child is being deliberately disobedient, consistency is vital. Identify the inappropriate behavior and also define and acknowledge appropriate behavior. According to Denis Donovan, M.D. and Deborah McIntyre, MA, RN in their excellent book, *What Did I Just Say?* parents need to acknowledge even reluctant compliance. "If you want the compliant behavior to become real, never discredit it...."

4. "What about a young child who is reacting angrily or with violence?"

For an answer to this question, we turn to Dr. Peter Goldenthal. Dr. Goldenthal warns that when a child repeatedly "acts out" violently or with disproportionate anger (when the behavior is clearly and repeatedly inappropriate), it is time to seek help for the child and for the family. However, when a child reacts angrily on occasion or it appears to be an understandable, but severe, response to circumstances, then the parent should intervene. Angry expressions addressed to siblings, parents, teachers, or others almost always indicate a failure of communication. Yet angry expressions usually do not give us any real information. A child who shouts, "I hate you!" is expressing failed communication, but not giving the parent any guidance.

For that reason, parents should consider breaking the pattern of anger and allowing time for the underlying issues to surface so that they can be discussed. For techniques to accomplish this, review the chapters on tag questions, presuppositions, and embedded suggestions. Dr. Wirth suggests sitting knee-to-knee with the younger child and holding his hands and looking into his eyes. In this way, you can command his attention and allow him to gain control of himself and to respond more appropriately.

In any case, probably the most powerful tool you have at your command is your own behavior. Be a great model. Become aware of your own anger and practice being able to acknowledge the anger, but calm your mind. Being angry is not conducive to great decision making. As children watch and hear you calm yourself, they will learn to do the same. This takes practice, but it can be done.

3

Frequently Asked Questions about Teenagers

"It is by believing in roses that one brings them to bloom."

—French proverb

1. "How do you handle teenage expressions of anger?"

The best solutions to teen anger involve creating a foundation by using the prenatal and postpartum techniques discussed in the earlier chapters. By modeling good problem solving skills, effective communication skills, and love, we minimize outbursts of anger. By exhibiting the ability to interrupt our own anger, we teach that skill to our children. Scientists call this period of negative emotion the "refractory period." However, while it is difficult to stop the effects of a negative emotion, there are many ways to interrupt this negative pattern.[24] By apologizing when we do succumb to anger, and by admitting our overreaction, we teach our children, by example, that there are better ways.

However, if you currently have a teenager who is expressing himself or herself angrily, you should begin by realizing that what is motivating his or her responses may not be anger at all. Rather, as children reach the ages of twelve to fifteen, they begin to assert their own personalities. If these expressions of independence are interpreted or labeled by you as anger, and if they are met with angry words, voice tones, or body language, the child (who may simply see their own behavior as an assertion of their independence) may be confused by your response. Or the child may simply be mirroring your own reaction to his or her expression of independence.

By adopting the belief that "The quality of my communication is the quality of the response I get," you may begin to become more tolerant of ordinary teenage behavior or more willing to try new and different approaches to communication.

When you tolerate acceptable assertions of independence, you make explosive "showdowns" less likely. Also, by injecting genuine humor, rather than the sarcasm which so permeates parent/teenage communication, you may find that you are creating a more positive environment in which communication can occur. Having said that, truly bad or rude behavior is unacceptable. Certain behaviors are unacceptable in most families and should bear consequences for the teen. Punishment unrelated to the tools needed by the teen to effectively interrupt his angry response will not get you the result you desire. Punishment must be linked to the negative behavior. Acknowledgment should be given when improvement, however incremented, is displayed. Tools and skills to help the teen succeed should be modeled by the parent. Consistency and boundaries are, therefore, important here.

Let's take a number of techniques independently, and consider how they may assist in dealing with a parent's reaction to teenage "anger." First, become more sensitive to the teen's situation. I am not suggesting surrendering your duties. However, learn to detect when you are moving toward a confrontation. When communicating with a teenager in a certain way does not seem to dissipate the anger, then don't continue to hammer away in the same manner. Consider other alternatives. Practice interrupting your own movement toward angry confrontation.

If a child is saying something clearly objectionable such as, "I hate you!" it is appropriate to say, "I don't like the way you are speaking to me. If you can think of another way to speak to me I would like to listen." My wife is a little tougher—she will just say, "Make yourself more appealing" when I am acting like an angry teen. That works on me.

In addition, remember to be "outcome-based" in your communication with teens. If you want a teenager to participate in family relationships, remember to approach the communication with that result clearly in mind. It is appropriate in dealing with teenagers to consider a *quid pro quo*. For example, if you desire that the teen be involved in family activities and the teen desires more personal time, or time with friends, you need to consider her request. You need to create, in the teenager's mind, reasons why the time with her family would be enjoyable for her or at least tolerable. One of those reasons could be that, by spending time with you, she will earn your continued respect in her judgment and you will recognize that she has a desire to spend time with friends that must also be met.

However, when a particular way of communicating or a suggestion does not get the result you want, it is important to avoid condemning the teenager and placing yourself in direct opposition to her. Instead, just realize that particular approach did not work at that time with that child. You have to be committed to continuing on and finding out what does work.

2. "What is the best way to approach my child about pre-marital sex, drinking, and drugs?"

This question reflects concern about behavior which may be physically or psychologically harmful to our children. Questions like this one generally arise at a time when a child is asserting her own independence and spending time with friends, going to concerts, and engaging in other activities which may expose her to inappropriate sex, drugs and alcohol. Her response to these situations is linked to her sense of self and to her relationship with you. There is significant evidence that children who spend more time with parents and/or who have higher self-confidence are much less likely to become involved in unsafe sex or drug and alcohol abuse.

For that reason, you should begin, as early as possible, to develop the child's self-esteem and confidence and the skills of good decision making. You should allow open lines of communication so that children of all ages feel comfortable approaching you. Again, we turn to Dr. Peter Goldenthal who stresses that teenagers need to be confident that they have an open line of communication. They need to feel that you *will* listen to them. Listening is not, however, according to Goldenthal, just a brief allocation of time. "Teenagers fall along a spectrum. Some will ask personal questions or relate intimate concerns very quickly. At the other end, some teens are remote and do not communicate well. However, for most teens, there is a lengthy process of becoming comfortable in stating their concerns." For this reason, extended opportunities for parent/teen communication should be provided. Most teens will not just launch into their most private concerns.

For parents who have multiple children, this is complicated by the eager listening ears of younger siblings. However, be aware of this need and do the best you can. Again, never discourage attempted communication, even if it is reluctant. If you want your children to share their thoughts and concerns, you must encourage every attempt.

Finally, remember to employ the skills of silence and listening. We have, in this country and culture, a well-intentioned compulsion to instruct. We feel that we know the answers and we want to save our children from the experience of our own painful errors. However, giving the solution often creates alienation or dependence. Remember to ask questions and allow the child time to work through his own answers and solutions.

If a child suggests a flawed solution consider asking, "Can you think of any advantages or disadvantages of that strategy?" "Are there other alternatives that might be better for you?"

With older teens, use their developing skills. When a teen wants to do something with which you may not agree, you might ask, "If you had a son or daughter and you were concerned about them, would you allow them to do this?" You may be surprised by the level of thinking you get in response, but be flexible and prepared for anything.

Appendix

4

Frequently Asked Questions about Adult Children and Grandchildren

"Don't curse the darkness—light a candle."

—Chinese proverb

1. "What about e-mail? I want more contact, but my children seem to misunderstand my e-mail messages."

E-mail has the disadvantage of being unidimensional. It allows the reader only one modality of perceiving your message. When you are speaking to a child, they are able to look you in the eye, assess your posture, your voice tone, and your intentions. They can judge from your words, as well as these other factors, the multiple levels of your meaning. However, when someone reads an e-mail he is generally repeating the words to himself and in his mind he inserts his own perceived tones and nuances.

E-mail also tends to be sloppy and quick. We can send an e-mail before we've had a chance to cool down. We can send an e-mail before we've had a chance to reflect. This makes e-mail even more subject to misinterpretation or unintended results.

The reader's state of mind may also have much to do with how she perceives your writing and the words you chose. For that reason, you may wish to limit e-mail to more factual sorts of updates and questions. More complex and emotional issues should be dealt with over the telephone or, better yet, in person. Generally, in e-mails you have to be extremely wary of using humor or sarcasm, as both are extremely difficult to convey through an e-mail because the reader lacks the ability to assess body language and other gestures which might soften the effect. Finally, allow a cooling-off period before sending an e-mail in response to something that has upset you. Better yet, consider making that phone call or, when possible, a personal visit.

2. "How do I improve my relationships with my adult children?"

Remember, the earlier you start establishing a great relationship with your children, the better. However, as Dr. Goldenthal observes, "It is never too late to start." In the case of adult children, you also need to remember that you can still do harm. You should avoid saying insidious things about one of your children to others. Whenever you speak that way about another party, it leaves your child wondering what you might be saying about him. Dr. Goldenthal also cautions that you should not make your children compete for your affection. Be careful how you reward communication with adult children just like younger children. If you pay attention to an adult child only when they complain bitterly, you are reinforcing that negative behavior. Rather, make sure that you pay attention and reward all appropriate contacts and communications.

Remember that raising children, and then maintaining a good relationship with them through adulthood, is a process. What worked at one stage of their lives will not necessarily work now. As children grow, marry, and have children of their own, their personal circumstances, desires, and the way in which they think, analyze and respond (their internal processes) may change. You have to remember the touchstone of flexibility and develop it in your relationships with your adult children. What worked before may no longer work. What excited that child may no longer excite him. Be inquisitive, respectful and aware of your children's interests. That will promote rapport and better communication.

Contrary to popular belief, opposites do not attract, and the skills of rapport discussed in Chapter 8 are always appropriate. Adult children will enjoy spending time with you, speaking with you on the phone, and dealing with you when they feel at ease with you. Employ the techniques of building and maintaining rapport.

Finally, remember to agree with your adult children even when you do not. Why? Establish areas of agreement first, and then explore the areas of disagreement. Agreement makes it more likely that your other points will be considered. There may be times when you have disagreements with your children, but use the techniques discussed in Chapter 12 on agreement for altering the uncomfortable portions of disagreeing. For example, when an adult child holds an opposing view to your own, you should adopt a portion of his own argument. If you acknowledge the valid points of his argument, you are likely to gain his respect. If you ignore all of his or her reasons he or she will almost instantaneously judge you to be taking an unreasonable position and be likely to ignore all remaining aspects of your argument. That does not advance your position.

You can reach agreement with your adult children by explaining to them what portions of their view seem correct, and acknowledging that you feel these are right. Only then should you ask them what would happen if they went along with your way of thinking, altered their view, or recognized better solutions. In this way, they will mentally consider altering their views or consider better solutions without hesitation because they need to go through that process before they can understand the nature of your question. Remember the suggestion, "Don't think of the color blue." You must think of it to understand the sentence. Furthermore, they are viewing you as supportive and your suggestions as cooperative, not in direct opposition to their own.

3. "How much should I tell my children about my wealth and estate planning?"

There is a broad range of views on this issue. As a trusts and estates attorney, I can tell you only the conclusions I have drawn by observing thousands of clients grapple with this decision. In my own case, I feel that age-appropriate honesty is the best policy.

Children of all ages want to know that their parents are thinking of them and providing for them, and they are usually respectful of their parents wishes. While, as a general rule, I think it is appropriate to tell a child or children that you have engaged in planning and to be a little bit more explicit with adult children, it is almost always a mistake to discuss the particulars of the plan with them.

Children bring their own views on these matters to the table, and the selection of one child over another as an executor or trustee (while perhaps highly rational) can create issues between the children during your lifetime that might not otherwise ever exist. Thus, specifics should generally be avoided, as they may cause problems, and you may wish to make changes over time.

As to the issue of disclosing wealth, you must exercise caution. If you wait too long to disclose your wealth, it can leave children unprepared to deal with it. If you disclose wealth to children too soon, it can create a sense of entitlement or dependence.

Generally, it is best to begin early to develop good thinking and decision-making skills in children so that they will have a high level of self-esteem and confidence. However, it is never too late to start and you should trust your gut.

4. "I don't like the way my children are bringing up my grandchildren. How can I communicate this without damaging our relationship?"

As with any disagreement, some basic rules apply. It is harder for people (even your children) to disagree with someone they like and respect. For that reason, all criticism, suggestions, and thoughts should be offered in a way that maintains their love and respect for you. You ultimately want them to consult you and act on your advice, or remain neutral about it—but not to ignore you.

You also need to realize and accept that they may not implement or enact many of your ideas. Be pleased if and when they do. Be prepared for when they do not. When they do ignore your advice there is a tendency for many people to ask themselves, "Why don't my children respect me?" Avoid the urge to label their decision a sign of disrespect. Instead, ask, "Are there reasons why it might not be possible for them to follow my advice? Why might they think or act differently?" If you want to equate their parenting decisions with disrespect that is a choice you can make. However, it is not an empowering choice. It will not enhance your relationship. Try to make choices that will enhance your time with your children and grandchildren.

You will also want to make use of outcome-based communication. Pick your battles. Do not disagree with your children on minor points. Next, build rapport and have a clear plan. Remember to be flexible. Questions or rejections are not a rejection of you. If an adult child tells you, "I cannot raise my child that way," then ask, "What would happen if you did?" This has the effect of making your child consider your suggestion. They cannot avoid this imaginary exercise.

Also, remember to listen. Many times, we are so intent on having an impact that we ignore the response to our suggestions. We keep hammering away. Remember to listen. Be prepared to apologize 1) if you are wrong; 2) if you have overstepped a reasonable boundary, or 3) even when you are improperly perceived by your child to have erred. I have spoken to a number of clients whose pride prevents them from apologizing to their child. Often, they have good rational reasons for their refusal. However, if your goal is to spend time with your children and grandchildren, and you are perceived by them as having done something wrong, the only way to your desired outcome may be to apologize. Don't sacrifice your relationships to pride. Apologize and begin to rebuild.

5. "What can I do to improve my relationship with my grandchildren?"

First, begin by realizing that your involvement with your grandchildren is mutually beneficial. They gain an insight into their own relationships with their parents by observing their parents interacting with you. By watching you, your grandchildren realize, perhaps unconsciously, that their parents are, themselves, children. Without interacting with you, they may never get this insight. Remember also that being with your grandchildren will revitalize you. They remind you of your own youth. They view things through fewer experiences and filters. Their views, reactions, and stories can be fascinating and hilarious.

Remember, your children may make different rules and distinctions than you did. Your grandchildren live in a different world. Be respectful of the differences. If all of your interactions with grandchildren lead to disputes with your own children, your times with the grandchildren will become less frequent or less wonderful.

As parents, we have certain responsibilities in raising our own children. We are their parents, we cannot just be their friends. You *can* however cultivate friendships as an aspect of your relationship with grandchildren. Dr. Peter Goldenthal observes, "Children are often disappointed if the grandparent relationship doesn't have a friendship quality. Grandchildren should be able to enjoy that relationship." In other words, it is okay to indulge grandchildren. Just be aware of the boundaries established by their parents.

6. "How can I foster relationships between, or among, my adult children?"

Your adult children are just that. They are your *adult* children. How they interact with one another will, by this time in your life, be pretty well established. However, having said that, there are ways in which parents can provide support designed to improve relationships between, or among, their children.

First, be aware that your children may have busy lives and many pressures. They believe that they live in another world, a world different and more difficult than your own. They may believe that you did not experience these sensations that they are having. Whether or not that is true, you must be aware of their perceptions.

Make the time that you spend with each child enjoyable. Create an opportunity for each of them to enjoy his time with you. Find out what each child likes about himself and about your other children. Share with each child how the other respects him. Siblings may or may not share this with one another. Tell them what the others enjoy. However, avoid telling your adult children insidious things about their siblings. It unconsciously leaves each child wondering about what you may be saying about him. You can encourage contact between children, but you cannot force it or control it.

Your physical distance from your children may impact how and when you can interact with them or how and when they interact. However, by establishing the best possible relationship you can with each of your children, you also encourage them to find pleasure in their family relationships, and this will hopefully extend to their own children and to their siblings.

Finally, Dr. Goldenthal says that adult sibling rivalry may be perpetuated in part because many parents make adult children continue to compete for their attention. When I asked Dr. Goldenthal how best to improve adult/sibling relationships knowing these things, his answer was simple: "Avoid doing them!" Dr. Goldenthal acknowledged that if you need to tell your children that you did these things and that you feel sorry in order for you to feel better, that is fine. However, absent that need, he advised parents of adult children to keep such things to themselves, stop engaging in the negative behavior and, when possible, share positive things that one child has said about another as a way of improving sibling relationships.

5

The Power
Parenting
Bibliography

This bibliography contains a number of resources, books and Web-based information for parents of children of all ages. For your convenience, the resources are arranged as follows 1) Expectant Parents; 2) Newborns through School Age Children; 3) Teenagers and Adults. As with any resources, you may personally find some, or all of these, to be credible and useful. However, the author and publishers are providing these resources based, in some cases, on the recommendations of parents or other advisors, and not on an independent review of the resources. As with any information, we encourage you to look for what is useful to you in each of these and to begin to apply and utilize what helps you improve your life as a parent and improve the world for your children.

1. Resources for Expectant Parents

Wirth F., MD. *Prenatal Parenting*. New York, NY: Harper Collins, 2001.

Gillett, R. *Change Your Mind, Change Your World*. New York, NY: Fireside Books, 1992.

Davis, M., Ph.D., Eshelman, E. and McKay, M., Ph.D. *Relaxation and Stress Reduction Workbook*. New York, NY, 1995.

Chopra, D. MD. *New Parent Creating Health*. Boston, Massachusetts: Houghton Mifflin, 1987.

2. Resources for Parents of Newborns through School Age Children

Faber A. and Mazlish, E. *How to Talk so Kids Will Listen and Listen so Kids Will Talk*. New York, NY: Quill, 2002.

Faber A. and Mazlish, E. *Between Brothers and Sisters: A Celebration of Life's Most Enduring Relationships*. New York, NY: Quill, 2002.

Goldenthal, P., Ph.d. *Beyond Sibling Rivalry*. New York, NY: Henry Holt, 1999.

Wallace, C. McD. *Elbows off the Table, Napkin in the Lap, No Video Games During Dinner—The Modern Guide to Teaching Children Good Manners*. New York, NY: St. Martins Griffin, 1996.

Donovan, D. MD and McIntyre, D. *What Did I Just Say— How New Insights into Childhood Thinking Can Help You Communicate More Effectively with Your Child*. New York, NY: Owl Books, 1999.

Connor, B. *Everyday Opportunities for Extraordinary Parenting*. Napperville, IL: Source Books, Inc. 2000.

Doe, M., Walch, M., Ph.D. *Ten Principals for Spiritual Parenting: Nurturing Your Child's Soul.* New York, NY: Harper Perrenial, 1998.

Armstrong, T. *Seven Kinds of Smart-Identifying* and *Developing Your Many Intelligences.* New York, NY: Ploom, 1993.

deBono, E. *deBono's Thinking Course.* New York, NY: Facts on File, 1994.

Pryor, K. *Don't Shoot the Dog!* New York, NY: Bantom Books, 1984.

Schulmann, M. *The Passionate Mind—Bringing up Intelligent and Creative Child.* New York, NY: The Free Press, 1991.

Mackenzie, R. Ed. D. *Setting Limits How to Raise Responsible, Independent Children by Providing Reasonable Boundaries.*

Goleman, D. *Emotional Intelligence.* New York, NY: Bantom Books, 1995.

3. Resources for Parents of Teens and Adults

Leeds, D. *The Seven Powers of Questions—Secrets to Successful Communication in Life and Work.* New York, NY: Perigee, 2000.

Arnot, R. MD. *The Biology of Success.* New York, NY: Little Brown and Company.

Root-Bernstein, R. and M. *Sparks of Genius: The Thirteen Thinking Tools of the Worlds Most Creative People.* New York, NY: Houghton Mifflin, 1999.

Dilts, R. and Epstein, T. *Dynamic Learning.* Capatola, CA: Meta Publications, 1995.

Leiberman, D. Ph.D. *Make Peace with Anyone*. New York, NY: St. Martins Press, 2002.

Michalko, M. *Cracking Creativity: The Secrets of Creative Genes*. Berkeley, CA: Ten Speed Press, 1998.

Finlayson, A. *Questions That Work*. New York, NY: American Management Association, 2001.

Cialdini, R., Ph.D. *Influence—The Psychology of Persuasion*. New York, NY: Quill, 1984.

Buzan, T. *The Mind Map Book*. New York, NY: 1993.

Bandler, R. *Magic in Action*. Capatola, CA: Meta Publications, 1992.

Ayan, J. *Aha! Ten Ways to Free Your Creative Spirit and Find Your Great Ideas*. New York, NY: Crown Trade Paperbacks, 1997.

Higgins, J. *101 Creative Problem Solving Techniques*. Winter Park, FL: The New Management Publishing Company, 1994.

Andreas, S. and C. *Change Your Mind and Keep the Change*. Moabb, UT: Real People Press, 1997.

Robbins, A. *Unlimited Power*. 1996.

Elgin, S. *The Gentle Art of Verbal Self Defense* and *More on the Gentle Art of Verbal Self-Defense*. Barnes and Noble Books, 1980.

Csikzentmihalyi, M. *Finding Flow*. New York, NY: Basic Book, 1997.

Appendix

6

Reading
Resources

1. Ohio State University's Extension Fact Sheet on reading which is available at http://Ohioline.osu.edu/hyg-fact/5000/5287.html.
2. *Reading to Children Is Essential* by Nikki Cavalier Rabel.
3. *parenthood.com* which has reading information and links.
4. Pediatric services at www.pediatricservices.com maintains a recommended reading list.
5. CTS Public Television page at www.KCTS.org/kids/children/index.asp is a great site with tips on reading to children.

Endnotes

1 George Korona, *Organizing and Memorizing* (New York: Columbia University Press, 1972)

2 Note: If you would like to examine an alternative way of thinking and learning, consider reading: *Lateral Thinking* and de *Bono's Thinking Course*, by Edward de Bono, and *Make the Most of Your Mind* and *The Mind Map Book* by Tony Buzan. These books are available through our Web site www.successtechnologies.com. If you register and join the Success Technologies community, you can also download a free Brain-Booster Bibliography.

3 Lawrence Katz, Ph.D. and Manning, Rubin, *Keep Your Brain Alive*, (New York: Workman Publishing) citing the research of Karl Lashley. See also Balevski, P. and Ganovski, L. "The Effect of Suggestion on Short and Long Term Memory." Suggestology 2, pp. 22-28.

4 Dr. Richard Bandler and John Grinder, *The Structure of Magic*, (Palo Alto, CA: Science and Behavior Books, Inc.).

5 NLP calls our attention to learning great behaviors by modeling others. However, we need to be good models for our children. A. Bandura, *Social Learning Theory* (Englewood Cliffs, N.J.: 1977). See also Katz and Manning ibid citing Dr. John Allman, "Tracing the Pathways for Linking Emotion and Reason," *New York*

Times, Dec. 6, 1994, and Anthony Damasio and Ralph Adolph's research at the University of Iowa linking emotion and memory enhancement.

6   Dr. Robert Arnot in his excellent book *The Biology of Success* encourages the reader to consider such factors as color, temperature and humidity, light, air quality, acoustics, aroma, dimensions, and clutter (or lack of same), in creating his optimal learning space.

7   This idea that when knowledge is synthesized or combined, it creates a "whole that is greater than the sum of its parts" is articulated in Gestalt theory and in Wundt's *Principle of Creative Results*. Wm. Wundt, *Outlines of Psychology* (Leipzig and Heidelberg, 1907).

8   Scientists studying critical linguistics have observed that the "structure of language we use encodes beliefs and values which in turn unconsciously affect our behavior and choices." R. Fowler, R. Hedge, G. Cress, and T. Trew, *Language & Control* (London: 1979).

9   The benefits and utility of this belief are explained more fully on pages 23 and 47.

10   *The Synaptic Self*, by Joseph LeDoux, examines, in detail, the concepts of brain chemistry, neuroscience and how these concepts have been employed by modern psychology to develop Cognitive Behavioral Therapy, (CBT). CBT has been used to successfully treat many nonpsychotic conditions including anxiety disorders and depression. In addition to fixing problems in human behavior we can use this knowledge to make ourselves feel better. If you want to feel better more often then

think the thoughts breathe, act, and use the posture you use when you feel great. This will trigger the neurotransmitters and brain-body chemistry to support you.

[11] The Crespi effect explains that increased performance results from increased incentives. In essence, your good feelings fuel even better results. LP Crespi, "Amount of Reinforcement and Level of Performance." *Psychological Review*, Vol. 4 (1944).

[12] For more informatin on the limits of verbal communication and other factors essential to effective communication see *Accelerated Learning* by Allyn Prichard, EdD and Jean Taylor citing stuides by Ray Birdwhistell, and *Memory and Learning Techniques* by Donald J. Lofland, PhD.

[13] Bandler and Grindler, the creators of NLP, have studied the models of great communicators and the effective methods employed by psychology, hypnosis, family therapy, and linguistics. For more information see www.successtechnologies.com for our NLP and Hypnosis Bibliography.

[14] This idea of "noise" and the limitations of language are examine by Alfred Korzbski in his writings on general semantics. For more information on general semantics visit www.general-semantics.org. An especially good article is entitled "Words and What They Do to You."

[15] In *10 Principles for Spiritual Parenting*, Mimi Doe and Marsha Walch, Ph.D., credit listening with encouraging the "unbounded creativity of children."

[16] Dr. Peter Goldenthal notes in his book *Beyond Sibling Rivalry* that "listening is something we can do for our children that produces immediate and long-lasting results."

[17] How do you check? I recommend actually asking. Now you can ask questions in a way that may offend or you can ask in a way that entertains. You can ask questions that are discreet and may not even be consciously noted. Be aware of what you're doing but ask. For example, if you say "Clean-up your room." to a young child you might then need to ask "When mommy says 'please clean up' does she want you to push everything under the bed?" With a teenager, you might say "Now I know that 'Clean-up' can mean many different things. What do you think I mean? This can be followed up again by restating the agreement. "So we agree that cleaning your room includes making the bed and taking out the trash."

[18] Now what if your child says "No. I can't remember." Then try asking, "What would happen if you did?" or "Can you imagine feeling good if you did?" Your child may not immediately give you the response you want. However, they will imagine the behavior and feeling good about it. That might be progress.

[19] For more information on understanding sub-modalities as described by NLP, and on improving your communication skills read *An Insider's Guide to Sub-Modalities*, by Richard Bandler and Will MacDonald.

[20] In *Dynamic Learning* by Robert B. Dilts and Todd A. Epstein, the authors examine the strategies used by great spellers.

[21] For a discussion of the limits of e-mail see the FAQ Appendix on e-mail and adult children and grandchildren.

[22] Notice, by the way, how much different it feels to say "I'm

miffed" or "I'm annoyed" when compared with "I'm angry!" Choose the words you say to yourself more carefully.

[23] For more age-appropriate information on reading and storytelling activities see our Reading Bibliography in Appendix Six.

[24] An interesting overview of western science and eastern philosophy on this issue is presented in *Destructive Emotions* by Daniel Goldman.

Index

ORDERING BOOKS

Benefits:
- This book makes a great gift for new moms and dads, expectant moms and dads and parents of teens
- This book is a great gift for anyone interested in improving his or her communication skills
- This book can be a great charitable or community fundraiser (see the next page)

If you'd like to order one or more books:

E-mail: dfrees@successtechnologies.com
Web: www.successtechnologies.com
Fax: 610-933-3603
Telephone Orders: 1-800-769-5454
Mail: Success Technologies, Inc.
                   P.O. Box 507, Malvern, PA   19355

ORDER FORM

BILL TO: _____   SHIP TO:_____

Name:_____   Name: _____

Address: _____   Address:_____

_____   _____

Telephone:_____   _____

_____ copies of *The Language of Parenting* at $14.95 each $ _____

Add 6% sales tax (PA residents) $ _____

Shipping ($3.50 for the first book, $2.50 for each additional book) $ _____

Total $ _____

☐ Check in the sum of $_____enclosed.
   Please make checks payable to: Success Technologies, Inc.

☐ Please charge to my credit card

☐ VISA   ☐MasterCard   ☐ American Express

Name on Card_____   Expiration Date _____

Account Number _____

Signature _____

HOST A GREAT CHARITABLE OR
COMMUNITY FUNDRAISER WITH
The Language of Parenting™

Success Technologies, Inc. and Red Wire Press have teamed up with David Frees, author and internationally known speaker, to create a great fundraiser. If you would like to run an entertaining, educational, and profitable fundraiser, call 1-800-769-5454 and ask for Nancy, Kate or David.

STI offers many fundraising options involving speeches, workshops, retreats or book sales with a substantial portion of all sales returned to your community, group or charity.

So, help your group, your community and the families within your group.

**Call 1-800-764-5454 or
e-mail: dfrees@successtechnologies.com today
to schedule a fundraiser.**

BECOME A *LANGUAGE OF PARENTING*™ PROVIDER AND TEACH COURSES

ADD A STREAM OF REVENUE TO YOUR EXISTING PRACTICE

If you are an allied healthcare provider, counselor, therapist, coach, social worker, child birth educator, or if you provide educational programs to parents and you are interested in teaching our *Language of Parenting*™ program,

Call 1-800-769-5454 or
E-mail: dfrees@successtechnologies.com

and ask how you can serve parents and children and add a new source of revenue to your practice or business.

TO HIRE DAVID FREES AS A SPEAKER OR FOR A SEMINAR, WORKSHOP, RETREAT OR CONFERENCE

CALL 1-800-769-5454

PROGRAM INFORMATION IS AVAILABLE BY E-MAILING

dfrees@successtechnologies.com

WHEN YOU HIRE DAVID FREES, YOUR PROGRAM WILL BE CUSTOMIZED, ENTERTAINING, INFORMATIVE AND EDUCATIONAL

TOPICS INCLUDE:

- The Language of Leadership: Building Ethical, Powerful and Persuasive Communication Skills™
- The Language of Parenting: Building Great Family Relationship at All Ages™
- Quantum Charisma: Building Relationships That Sell™
- The Power of Persuasion™
- Opening the Door to Charitable Giving™

CALL 1-800-769-5454